THE UNBEATABLES

Also by Richard O. Smith

The Man with His Head in the Clouds
James Sadler: The First Englishman to Fly

Oxford Student Pranks: A History of Mischief and Mayhem

Britain's Most Eccentric Sports

As Thick As Thieves: Foolish Felons and Loopy Laws

THE UNBEATABLES

RICHARD O. SMITH

Signal Books
Oxford

First published in 2015 by
Signal Books Limited
36 Minster Road
Oxford OX4 1LY
www.signalbooks.co.uk

© Richard O. Smith, 2015

The right of Richard O. Smith to be identified as the author of this work has been asserted by him in accordance with the Copyright, Design and Patents Act, 1988.

All rights reserved. The whole of this work, including all text and illustrations, is protected by copyright. No parts of this work may be loaded, stored, manipulated, reproduced or transmitted in any form or by any means, electronic or mechanical, including photocopying and recording, or by any information, storage and retrieval system without prior written permission from the publisher, on behalf of the copyright owner.

A catalogue record for this book is available from the British Library

ISBN 978-1-909930-27-8 Paper

Cover Design: Tora Kelly
Typesetting: Tora Kelly
Cover Images: © 369 Productions Limited

All still images © 369 Productions Limited; p.1 jorgen mcleman/ shutterstock; chapter headings Miguel Angel Salinas Salinas/ shutterstock

Printed and bound in Great Britain by TJ International Ltd, Padstow, Cornwall

The Unbeatables novel is based on the film *The Unbeatables* (U) starring Rupert Grint, Rob Brydon, Anthony Head, Peter Seranfinowicz, Eve Ponsonby, Ralf Little, Alistair McGowan, Stanley Townsend, Alex Norton, Darren Boyd, David Schneider, Simon Greenall, Andrew Knott, Jonathan Pearce. Screenplay by Michael Smith, Richard O. Smith, Juan José Campanella. Storyline Eduardo Sacheri, Gaston Gorali, Axel Kuschevatzky, Juan José Campanella. Inspired by "Memoirs of a Right Winger" by Roberto Fontanarrosa. Produced by Victor Glynn and David Burgess of 369 Productions. Directed by Juan José Campanella. Sound Director Nick Angell.

The author wishes to thank
James Ferguson, Victor Glynn, Oliver Ledbury, Mark Steel

This book is dedicated to everyone who follows their local team - wherever they are.

History does not record the identity of our planet's first footballer. Or the name of the first ever goalscorer. We don't know when or which of our pioneering ape ancestors first uttered the triumphant cry of…"Goal!"

Followed seconds later by the first scream of…"Offside!!"

And shortly afterwards by: "Referee, are you blind?!!!"

We don't know who choreographed the first goal celebration. Nor who came up with the first piece of post-match punditry. "Well, Gary, like zoo procedure following an escape, you have to ask some serious questions of the apes' keeper there."

But we do know that from that Saturday forth - and it WOULD have been a Saturday when football was created - mankind would no longer be devoid of a purpose. Never again would places where men meet fall silent due to a lack of conversational topic. From that day forth no one would ever fall over again without optimistically raising their arm for a penalty. And never again would primitive man be around at weekends to do his share of the cavework.

God may have created man, but man created football - and with it: his destiny.

From this point forward, mankind didn't re-set his goals, he created them for the first time. At a regulation eight metres apart.

So on the 8th day God created football. That's because he/she took the 7th day off to have a proper think about inventing something really useful this time; some of his previous creations were OK, but do we really need that much ocean?

In football God and mankind had combined to invent the Beautiful Game. And with it they had invented destiny, hope, ambition, glory and the offside trap.

"I think he's ready," announces Matty's mother, handing her husband a cup of tea. She mutes the TV showing *2001 Space Odyssey*, cutting off Richard Strauss' waltz mid-swirl.

"I don't know. It's such an important thing," Matty's father replies, obliviously spooning several sugars into his tea. "He might still be too young," he adds cautiously.

"Nonsense. It's time he knew. Don't you think he has a right to know?"

"Yes... er... no... I mean... yes, but er..." stutters his father, so distracted that he continues to heap more spoonfuls of sugar into his mug.

"Trust me," replies Matty's mother, giving her husband a steely look that clearly communicates: "this decision cannot be reversed, overturned or discussed further." Matty's father is used to recognising *that* look.

"Alright," he says resignedly, taking a sip of tea and immediately spitting it out.

"Nine sugars? Since when have you been a builder?" asks Matty's mother.

"OK, here's the plan," announces Matty's dad with rising enthusiasm detectable in his voice. "I'll go and have The Big Talk with Matty and you make me another tea - this one's too sweet for some reason. You're right, it's time to reveal the truth to him."

Matty is in bed but far from asleep.

"Are you still awake?" asks his father, rather unnecessarily.

Matty is motionless, pretending to sleep under the duvet,

but his pretence is as precarious as a 1-nil lead. His father starts to swivel back towards the door when Matty's deception is blown by an electronic voice proclaiming, "Penalty-kick awarded to the Stripes."

"Hmm… someone appears to be playing a virtual football game under the bed sheets. Even though we agreed no computer games after 9pm."

Even though he has been caught red-handed playing his football game after bedtime, Matty tries to appear innocent.

"I'm so sl-ee-py," he groans, yawning between each syllable for added sl-ee-py emphasis. It is an almost convincing performance of amateur dramatics.

"OK then, I'll let you sleep," his father says, allowing a teasing pause just long enough for Matty to think he has got away with his ruse, before adding, "so if you're sleepy you won't need this." Quickly he moves forward and grabs the boy's laptop, attempting to confiscate computer and football game. Pulling a newborn baby from a mother's hands would have been an easier task. And certainly met with less resistance.

"No!" yells Matty, "Give me that back! You'll ruin it! The Stripes are 4-3 up with only ten minutes to go."

I thought you were sl-ee-py," says his dad, mimicking his son's triple-syllabled emphasis.

"What? Oh, er… yeah," says Matty, busted for the second time in quick succession.

"But since you are clearly wide awake, your mother… and me… yeah me too, as I have equal input into decisions and don't just take orders from the skirt wearer in this marriage…"

"…get on with it!" calls out a female voice from the hallway.

"Sorry, yes I will." He pauses, as if carefully crafting the words to form his next sentence. "Listen, Matty, your mother and I have been planning to tell you something ever since you were very small. Now you are on the way to becoming an adult it's time to talk about some very grown-up things. Some facts about how you came to be who you are…"

"If it's about the birds and bees, mum already told me. And you're disgusting."

"Really? When? No, it's not about that. In fact, this might be even more important than that subject."

"Believe me, you're not an expert on that subject," interjects the female voice from the hallway.

"Shouldn't you be making more tea? I've got this," says Matty's father on the edge of sternly. Drawing a deep, exaggerated breath, he lets out a sigh for dramatic effect. Then he begins to recount the story that he and his wife have decided it is finally time to impart to Matty. "The story starts a long, long time again. Are you lying comfortably… not too comfortably as I don't want you falling asleep while I tell you the most remarkable story you will ever hear…"

"Look dad, I'm tired."

"Ok, we'll just take this laptop away and allow you to sleep while I'll finish the game for you."

"No, stop it!" protests Matty, "You're not qualified to play football. You're an Arsenal fan, remember!"

Matty's father spots a winning move in the negotiations. "OK then, I'll return the game for you to finish tomorrow, as long as you listen to my story."

"Don't you think I'm a bit old for a bedtime story, dad?"

Undaunted by Matty's response, his father begins his tale. "Once upon a time… I heard that groan… in a lovely little village like ours, with a village green like ours, with a quaint ancient church like ours, with a threatened post office like ours, with a charming if chaotically run café just like ours… I can tell you're only pretending to be asleep."

"Fair do's," says Matty.

"There was a boy who was mad on football… just like our boy. This story starts with him in the village's café where he's working as an after school job. By the way, this boy looks just like you. And he behaves like you. He's shy and sensitive, not a show-off. His head is often filled with daydreams - mainly dreams about football. He's softly spoken and quite slight. Let's say he easily gets shoved off the ball. Oh, and did I mention he's mad about foosball?"

This young boy is called Amadeo and right now he is carrying a tray with two ice-creams.

Regulars Moxey and Spencer are in the café as usual, sitting at a table they have occupied since before anyone can remember - some suspect before the café was built around them on this site. Every week they complete their football pools coupon at the same table but have never won a penny.

Not that it's hard for the villagers to imagine what the café must have looked like when it was built, as nothing appears to have been changed over the decades since - Including the tablecloths. The pot plants were last watered, and the walls last painted when the FA Cup Final was normally a contest between Blackpool and Preston North End. From a similar era are the garishly iced buns displayed under a perspex dome on the counter; their sell-by date so old it is probably written in Roman numerals. Pennants from an age when Wolverhampton Wanderers were the dominant British team in Europe are displayed on the walls. An enormous twin-blade fan rotates on the ceiling, like a helicopter attempting to lift the café airborne.

Whereas Moxey, Spencer and the others don't always seem to have much of a life of their own, the café's jukebox definitely does. As badly wired as a recalled cheap Christmas toy, this decrepit machine has a habit of randomly selecting songs and jumping tracks midway through playing them.

Pride of place in the café is given to the foosball table. Demonstrating his dedicated affection to foosball, Amadeo has lovingly hand-painted the two teams: one resplendent in green and yellow stripes he has fittingly christened the Stripes. Their perennial opponents are the Clarets. The foosballers look so realistic it is easy to imagine them being living breathing footballers - with real personalities. Amadeo can sometimes be spotted conversing with his creations as if he has befriended them.

Amadeo has even named some of the players. The Stripes are led by their talismanic captain Skip. Skip has a big heart and engine - full of stamina and enthusiasm to lead his boys by example. To Skip the team is everything - anything else is filed under "D" for distraction. As it can lead to "D" for defeat.

Midfielder Rico is a flair player, the flamboyance of his playing style matched by his exuberant hair. He revels in exhibiting his creativity both on the football field as well as at the hairdressers. Brothers in big hair, Rico is a mainstay of the Stripes' midfield alongside the dreadlocked Loco. Known for espousing Buddhist-light philosophy and his own unique Loco-isms, Loco is often heard "verbally squirting the foam of rationality onto the heated fires of on-the-field bust-ups" - as Loco himself once described, er, himself.

Fellow key players in the Stripes are identical twins the Bevilles - deliberately painted by Amadeo to look indistinguishable - alongside Korean midfielder Psy Kick, fullback partnership Stevie and Jono and all on his own on the back stick – or back rod: Mac the Keeper. Mac has been accessorised by Amadeo to always wear a cap.

The Stripes' opponents are led by burly no-nonsense-taken nor no-fools-suffered-gladly Gregor. Resplendent in a Claret shirt he leads and organises his Claret teammates. Their work rate is stupendous. Gregor's dream as a leader, Amadeo imagines, is to cut out any fancy flair and sign another defender. What his side lacks in ball-playing artistry, they make up for in industry. If the Stripes are giving 110% in a game, Gregor will demand his men give 111%. Mathematical implausibility doesn't concern him - beating the Stripes does.

Both the Stripes and Clarets are a little chipped and imperfect, their missing paintwork a proud badge of honour like scars from their duels - souvenirs from their epic tussles over all the years they have been pitted against each other.

Old-fashioned it may be, but the village is fond of this eccentric place and its eccentric owner, a giant man-mountain-range known simply as the Guv'nor. It is underperforming, underfunded and under threat of modern corporate competition, but it is the village's very own café and the regulars support it affectionately like they would a local football club.

This is how it has always been: the regulars, the malfunctioning jukebox, the smell of frying chips… and the foosball table. And in foosball, like life, there is no close season.

Only one thing is obviously different today. There is a stranger in the café. A mysterious man sits on his own observing the scene. He is enormously fat and wearing an oversized and expensive coat that struggles to contain his generous girth. He appears suspiciously out of place. He also looks like he is waiting for something to happen - which it rarely does in this trickling backwater.

Just now the Guv'nor, has prepared the ice-cream order for Amadeo to take to Table Five.

"OK, I'm on my way," Amadeo calls to the Guv'nor, carefully balancing the tray and its contents above his head as he weaves between the tables. But suddenly he stops dead in his tracks, frozen as if put into a trance by a stage hypnotist.

"Hi there!"

The temporarily mesmerised, statue-like Amadeo does not respond. He is lost for words.

"Are you OK?"

The questioner is a girl known as Lara. Sure, Amadeo has seen girls before, but this is the first one he has really noticed. And this is the first time that she has spoken to Amadeo, though she often comes into the café for an afterschool ice-cream treat.

With her is her younger brother Chester, plump, short-sighted and distinctly clumsy.

"You're melting," Lara observes casually.

"Oh yes," replies Amadeo, sounding more like a dog advertising insurance than a cool boy comfortable with girls. "I know I'm melting," he says feebly before retreating back into silence.

"The ice cream," Lara points out. Realising further explanation is required, she adds, "the ice cream on the tray you're carrying... it's melting onto your front."

"Oh yeah, I'd better take this to Table Five."

"We're Table Five," says Lara.

"Um... oh yeah, so you are," stammers Amadeo, really wishing he could be cooler right now. He puts down the ice-creams with a shaky hand.

Moving away from Table Five, Amadeo feels an irresistible compulsion to turn around and glance at Lara. She's wearing a knitted hat the colour of strawberry ice-cream and her sweater is the blushing pinkish red shade of Turkish delight. Her hair has a dark purple, blackcurrant tint. Her jacket is the warm orange colour of marmalade and snug winter fires. She smells of milk chocolate and Christmas cookies. Amadeo thinks she looks delicious.

Even young Chester, not in possession of the most sharpened intellect, is capable of spotting Amadeo's obvious backwards look. Unwisely he reacts by taunting his sister, chanting, "Lara's got a boyfriend, Lara's got a boyfriend!" Lara retaliates to the derision by landing a firmly applied back-hand to her brother's chops. "Owwwruuuchhh!!!" Chester shrieks, before going down to earth like an Italian centre-forward fouled in the penalty area. "Lara hit me! Lara hit me!" he whines, "Lara raised her arms! Straight red card for Lara, surely?!" Chester goes down clutching both his face and leg.

Lara and Amadeo ignore Chester's performance. Referees have to endure more bad acting than professional casting directors - and Chester is certainly playacting here; Lara barely caught him. Amadeo wants to tell Lara that her brother "went down far too easily". Yet for some reason he cannot. Shyness is acting like an invisible force field, depriving him of the ability to speak. He appears momentarily lost in a dream, oblivious to his surroundings. Until now his interests and dreams have been dominated by his twin obsessions: football and foosball. But seeing Lara has hatched a new feeling within him.

"Looks like Amadeo may have to find room for a third interest," muses Spencer to Moxey, observing Amadeo's frozen state.

"How about predicting this match," suggests Spencer, "a match in the village between Amadeo and Lara?"

"For me," says Moxey, "the boy Amadeo needs to impose himself much more, his frailties are starting to show. Opportunities at this level are few and far between, and when he comes up against a superb outfit like Lara's…"

"Her cardigan/hat/scarf combo does work well…"

"Exactly, Spencer, that scarf is right out of the top drawer. Amadeo's own outfit is lacking in comparison. He's got to up his game considerably to have any sort of chance of turning this around and getting a result with Lara. When an opening like this comes his way he has to react much better and make it count. And you have to say that was a tame effort by the lad. And a poor first touch. He'll be disappointed with that if he sees it again, he needs to express himself better and showcase his quality. Lara is a different class. At the end of the day his approach play is all wrong, his tactics unsound. The lad's been punished for being indecisive, and naivety at this level will cost him. He's got to start asking her questions. And giving a better account of himself. He must learn from this setback if he hopes to be there or thereabouts and win her. Lara will prove hard to break down."

"And how would you describe his defence for not serving the ice cream quicker, Moxey?"

"His delivery was poor. Schoolboy defending from the, er, schoolboy defender. At the end of the day, Amadeo is over the moon about being paired with Lara but he's not going to progress to the next round unless he improves dramatically. He's completely out of his depth. Got no chance whatsoever. Best he can hope for is if the manager decides to pull him off at half-time."

"So what's your prediction, Moxey?"

"They'll get married."

Amadeo is aware for the first time that he hosts an affection for Lara. Especially since she has now come and stood closer to him than any girl has previously done. So close he can smell her scent. She smells of lovely things: meadow flowers and lemon blossom, summer walks and Turkish delight. Instinctively he flinches away - after all a lifetime of determined shyness has left him unaccustomed to a female being this physically near to him. He has also just seen her flatten her brother with a foul that a 1970s Leeds United side would have considered unnecessarily dirty play. But then something strange happens. He begins to jettison his customary cautiousness, moves towards Lara, leans towards her. Her top lip forms the shape of a perfect Cupid bow. It looks like Amadeo is going to receive his first ever proper kiss. He anticipates the imaginary sound of a stadium celebrating his accomplishment. This would be amazing if he kissed Lara. Why is telling a girl or boy that you like them one of the hardest things to do? If they don't like you back then you risk scorn, stinging rejection and awkward silences. Surely Lara is going to kiss him. It looks like she will. Until... they both stop one second before the kiss, startled by the crashing opening of the café's main door.

There stands Young Flash, dramatically silhouetted by a blindingly bright light behind him.

Like a nurse or banker, accountant or decorator, you can tell what Young Flash does just by looking at him; and his profession is one thing: full-time bully. Before he says a word

Young Flash speaks through his body language, which is notably loud. He struts aggressively, puffing out his chest. Everything about him appears dark: his hair, eyes, jacket, trainers and, of course, his soul. His face bears an expression permanently set to "sneer". Indeed he comes complete with the whole bully package: jabbing fingers, cruel searching eyes and arms rippling with muscles. He gives the assembled villagers a look as sharp as a mosquito's bite.

"OK, you can tell your brother to turn his car headlights off now. That was the entrance I was after," he barks at one of the three minions in his bully boy entourage.

Flash snaps his fingers and a henchboy tosses him a football. After skilfully catching the ball with the back of his neck, Flash rolls it down his spine, then nonchalantly flicks it over his head with a deft back-heel. Relishing the opportunity to demonstrate his impressive keepy-uppy skills - alternating between left and right feet - Flash shows off his tricks, grandstanding to the café's customers.

Silence has settled over the café - mainly because one of Young Flash's henchboys has run ahead and unplugged the jukebox. "Oi, plug that back in, you toerag!" orders the Guv'nor. Ignoring his instruction, but not his threat, the aforementioned toerag scuttles away and cowers behind Young Flash.

"I have an announcement to make," declares Young Flash. Waiting until he has the entire attention of the room, he then clears his throat and announces in his most pompous voice, "'I'm a…"

"… Barbie Girl…" blasts out of the speakers. The Guv'nor has chosen the optimum moment to plug back in the jukebox.

Patiently awaiting his opportunity until he can pounce like a predator, the henchboy again tugs out the jukebox lead just as the Guv'nor has returned to his place behind the counter. Young Flash is keen to exploit the returning silence before it evaporates again. "No, I meant to say I am… I am about to sign youth forms with the biggest football club in our area!"

13

But no one is listening anymore. As the Guv'nor once more plugs in the jukebox, *Bigmouth Strikes Again* appropriately wafts through the speakers. Young Flash reacts by clicking his fingers, and pointing to the jukebox - summoning a loyal henchboy to unplug it yet again. The gigantic frame of the Guv'nor, now standing guard over the jukebox's power point, immediately persuades the henchboy to refuse his master's directive.

But Young Flash, always looking for trouble, has spotted something else. "Oh look, if it isn't the Football Champ? It's Amadeo - always playing with 'himself." The henchmen dutifully fold into laughter.

With Young Flash and his sidekicks' threatening entry into the café Amadeo has quietly positioned himself behind his beloved foosball table. Shyly looking down, he hopes - really hopes - that they will just go away. But bullies never do just go away.

Close by, a darkly-attired Emo Kid, the gloomy music of a band probably named Punish Your Parents leaking from his headphones, is playing a game on his tablet. Until, that is, one of Flash's henchboys deliberately kicks a football in his face. "On yer head, son! Ha ha ha!" chorus the henchboys.

Meanwhile the plump Chester, who has been nursing a precautionary handkerchief on his nose after being walloped in the face by his sister, announces "the bleeding's stopped!", only to be whacked in the face again - this time by Flash's expertly kicked football. "Oh, my nose is now bleeding again. I gave the all-clear too soon," he whimpers.

"Oi, you know you can't play football in here!" yells the Guv'nor.

"I don't think so. There's a sign outside on the village green saying 'No ball games', but there isn't one inside here," replies Young Flash defiantly. Gill Etre, a conservatively dressed older lady with a latte froth moustache covering her own moustache, is moved by Young Flash's odious antics to remark, "ce garçon est une douleur dans le derrière - if you pardon my French."

But Young Flash has Amadeo in his sights, like a lion spotting a gazelle supping at a watering hole. Amadeo instinctively goes to hide behind his beloved foosball table, but there is no escape.

"So think you can take me on at table football, do you?" Young Flash taunts Amadeo.

"Er…n…n…no. It's OK. Thank you," replies Amadeo shyly.

"Oh, so the toy football champion is scared."

Lara recognises a bully when she sees one, and she is seeing one right now. "Go away. We're minding our own business. This is a bully free zone."

"Wow, the toy football coward has got himself a feisty girlfriend. He's got a girlie for a coach, everyone."

His minions laugh on cue. "Yeah, he's got a girlie for a coach!" chortle the henchboys, evidently incapable of hosting original thoughts of their own.

"Leave us alone, you non-entity!" Lara says defiantly, before adding. "Your henchboys don't intimidate us."

"We're henchmen. Not henchboys," says one of the, um, henchboys.

"Henchboys!" Lara reiterates, savouring the way the word gives the henchboys an electric shock of annoyance every time she deploys it.

One of Young Flash's henchboys whispers into his boss's ear. Flash is not amused at the message and snaps back: "I know that 'non-entity' is an insult… whatever it means!" and ushers his henchboy away. "Really, some people just don't appreciate how difficult it is being a monstrous bully, especially with the appalling staff I have to work with."

He glares at Amadeo again. "Come on you coward and take me on. You will lose, of course."

Amadeo looks downwards at his magnificently painted foosballers, and grabs two of the foosball table's handles for comfort.

"So are you going to talk to them?" taunts Flash, emitting an evil laugh as he struts towards the table.

But he is surprised to find his route suddenly blocked by a very fat man with a very thin pencil moustache - as if he is compensating for his huge frame by permitting himself only a tiny moustache. Light flashes from his golden teeth whenever he speaks with a noticeably mid-Atlantic drawl. His snakeskin coat, lined with baby panda fur, is barely big enough for his padded frame. He is the stranger who has been silently watching events unfold.

"May I offer to hold coats, jackets and hoodies for you and your associates, sir, while you get down to business?" enquires the generously girthed gentleman. A sparkling and dazzling golden smile ensues. "Er, thank you," says Young Flash, momentarily confused and unsure. He does not know what the fat man wants but he knows he wants something. He is naturally suspicious - he assumes everyone is as nasty as himself - but he is intrigued by the clothes, the gold teeth, the accent…

"Roll the first ball into play," he snaps, "let battle commence. Or rather, let Amadeo's total humiliation and annihilation commence!"

Hushed customers form a ring around the foosball table to watch the showdown shootout between Young Flash and Amadeo. The theme from *The Good, The Bad and The Ugly* magically appears on the café's jukebox. A church bell tolls in the distance. Moxey and Spencer remove their hats. The Guv'nor crosses himself. The erratic jukebox changes to another spaghetti western theme, *A Fistful of Dollars*, signifying the shootout is about to begin. The stranger lights an enormous cigar and says in a voice similar to Clint Eastwood's: "Get three coffees ready."

With trembling fingers, Amadeo places the ball through the hole in the table's side and releases it onto the pitch. It is instantly followed by a sinister sound - a metallic "pling!" reverberation - ringing out throughout the café. It is the noise the ball makes when hitting the back of Amadeo's goal. "1-nil to the genius that is me," declares Young Flash. Next ball - if you've got any balls." His henchboys laugh mockingly. Amadeo carefully pushes the second ball into play, whereupon it is immediately despatched into his goal again. "2-nil", announces

Young Flash in his most arrogant voice. "Tell me," he continues, "are you planning to touch the ball at any stage?" A third ball is rolled into play, and a third goal is instantaneously scored by Young Flash. "Hmm. Given you play with yourself all the time I'd have thought you would have more strength in your wrists," he sneers.

Lara has witnessed enough, and feels for Amadeo's humiliation. "Amadeo, you're not even trying. It doesn't matter if you lose, but it matters if you don't even try. Go on, please try." Then she leaves a deliberate pause, so that Amadeo will realise that what she says next has been considered, not just a random heat-of-the-moment remark. "Try for me."

"I think I'll just use one hand now, like my opponent's love life!" trills Young Flash. His henchboys laugh like a pack of mocking hyenas - and smell as bad as them too. Amadeo releases the next ball, but this time flicks the ball between all five of his midfielders with incredible speed and dexterity. He passes to his inside-right who arrows the ball into Young Flash's vacant net. Amadeo's opponent, along with his henchboys, is suddenly as mute as a monk observing a monastic silence. Lara approaches Young Flash and opens her mouth to speak. "Hmm, forget what I was going to say," she says softly and appears to walk away, before suddenly spinning around and yelling, "Oh yes, it's come back to me now… GGGOOOOOOOOOAAAAAAAAAAAALLLLLLLL!!!!!!!! Back of the onion bag, my son!! El netto!!!"

Amadeo places the next ball into play. After some incredible eye-popping trickery, his players demonstrating technical foosball moves known as bounce passes, turnaround passes, and lane-angled passes, a loud "pling!!" reverberates around the café to signify another goal. Amadeo 2 Young Flash 3.

Young Flash is again stunned into silence. "You should be quiet more often. It really suits you," remarks Lara.

"Shut up, loser. And tell your loser boyfriend to release the next ball."

Amadeo does just that, and after some Ronaldo-like trickery, cleverly angles the ball into the goal for the equaliser.

Lara cannot stop another war cry of "GGGOOOOOOOAAAAAAAAAAALLLLLL!!!" bursting out of her.

"You can just say 'goal', you know," suggests one of Flash's henchboys somewhat pathetically. For that he receives a slap to the back of his head from head bully Young Flash.

"That's 3-3. Shall we call it a draw?" offers Amadeo sportingly.

"No. Next ball wins. You need to be shown that no one ever beats Flash. As I am one of the unbeatables!"

"OK then, if you insist there has to be a loser." Amadeo's fingers propel the ball through the slot where it rolls spinning into the middle of the table. The seventh and deciding ball is in play. Young Flash is angling his midfielders back and forth, like All Blacks performing an intimidating haka dance.

Amadeo concentrates. "Stop time wasting and get on with it - you're just delaying your inevitable defeat, loser!" shouts Young Flash.

"He's not time-wasting. It's called 'thinking'. You wouldn't recognise it," responds Lara.

Amadeo immediately claims possession, then instigates a passing sequence of such astonishing speed, skill and accuracy that Young Flash's brain barely has time to compute the information he is receiving from his eyes. A fraction of a second later the ball is fired low, hard and clinically into the corner of the goal. Young Flash's goalkeeper is oblivious to the white goalbound missile that just rocketed past his shoulder.

Calmly and sedately Lara walks towards Young Flash, her diminutive being unintimidated by the assembled bullies. She draws a long deep breath. What Young Flash mainly sees next are her tonsils as she shrieks "4-3!!!!!!!"

The café's customers murmur their collective approval at the outcome.

But Young Flash is less pleased. He reacts to his defeat by kicking an unfortunate chair, then an unfortunate henchboy - both make a loud noise as they clatter to the floor. Completing his hat-trick of dirty kicks, Flash then opts to kick the jukebox. The machine immediately plays the Beatles song *I'm A Loser*.

Scarlet with rage, Young Flash flounces out of the café, taking care to scream, "I never lose! That doesn't count 'cos I never lose!" His departure is hastened by the helping boot of the hefty Guv'nor. The jukebox is now playing Queen's *Another One Bites the Dust*.

Running onto the village green, with his henchboys loyally following like a pack of scruffy stray dogs, Flash picks up a discarded can and lobs it at the village's "Best Kept Village" sign, followed by some sharp stones. The henchboys follow their master's lead, picking up nearby stones and throwing them at the same target. Most miss, unlike Flash. "I really must surround myself with better henchmen," he says under his breath. "One day I may have a really important job to be done, and this rabble just won't cut it." He hurls another rock at the sign, the metallic clang testifying to the shot's remarkable accuracy.

"I hate this stupid village," he bellows, throwing a further stone between each word for emphasis. I WANT TO DESTROY THIS PLACE FOREVER!!! I'll teach them that Flash never loses. I'll win when I reduce this Retardville to rubble!"

Nearby the well-dressed, corpulent man is smoking a gigantic cigar. Nobody has noticed him leaving the café in the aftermath of the match. He blows a plume of smoke upwards, then approaches the gang. "Here are your coats, boys." Young Flash snatches his hoodie. His henchmen mimic his behaviour - rudely tugging back their jackets without acknowledging the stranger.

"So, are you hurting inside, kid?" asks the man.

"What's it to you, fatso?" replies Young Flash.

"Yeah, what's it to you, fatso? Ouch!" A henchboy's parroted question is curtailed by a quick slap to the back of the neck from Young Flash.

"Does defeat feel like a burning sensation in your stomach, as if acid has leaked in a ship's hull?" There is a silent pause, during which the stranger computes that Young Flash and his henchboys don't really do metaphors or similes.

"I think it's a good thing to see that you care about losing a foosball match so much," continues the stranger. "I can tell you're a natural footballer. To lose like that, you must have been as sick as a parrot with the norovirus."

"I didn't lose," says Young Flash.

"Good boy. Passion and a dogged determination to not accept reality are dual skills that could take you far, son. How would you like to be a star?"

"Who are you anyway?" asks Young Flash, his anger slowly giving way to curiosity.

"I'm known as the Agent. I used to be known as Mr. Fixer, but that looked bad whenever I was called as a witness for trials involving match fixing. Especially when the court usher said 'Call Mr. Fixer…'"

"Well, I don't need an agent. So Mr. Fixer has met his match." Flash is unaware he has made an accidental joke. His henchboys look worried, unsure whether to laugh for their master or not.

"You're right. You're clearly happy staying in this - how did you just describe it? - 'stupid village I hate so much'. So, I'll allow you to stay here then. No need to sign for a world famous football club. See you around, kid."

"A world famous club?" Young Flash has just realised what the stranger said.

"That's right. I have contacts with all the world's biggest clubs: Dynamo Bikelight, Real Messi, Athletico Margate, Buy A Lebkuchen, Interbred Milan, Wet Spam United."

"Wow, Wet Spam United? The Spammers?" Cool Young Flash cannot disguise the fact that he is caught suddenly starstruck.

"Your Arsenals, Chelseas, Liverpools, Gainsborough Trinitys - I have contacts at them all, kid."

Young Flash beams silent admiration towards the man.

"And I also have a pen if you'd like to sign with me," says the Agent smoothly.

Many years may have passed but the village looks the same. That's just how the villagers like it.

The same characters inhabit the café. Maybe a bit greyer, balder and fatter, but all completely recognisable nonetheless. Spencer and Moxey are still doing their weekly pools syndicate. "Now then, Mystic Moxey, it's time to gaze into your crystal football and predict the outcomes of the following games on this week's coupon. Manchester United v. Stockport County." "Hmm…" ponders Moxey, "away win." Spencer marks it down on the coupon as a win for the visitors. "Arsenal v. Accrington Stanley?" "That's an easy one. Away win," predicts Moxey. "Next fixture: Chelsea v. Frinton Sea Scouts under 13's 2nd XI?" Again, Moxey's footballing brain churns into action. After a lengthy pensive pause he declares confidently: "Away win." Spencer asks Moxey to prophesise another outcome. "Predict this one. A World Cup qualifier. Scotland at home to the unpopulated island of Herm, a place so small that corners have to be taken from well into Guernsey?" "Away win," responds Moxey. "And your final question: what makes the sound zub, zub, zub?" "A bee flying backwards," answers Moxey.

Close by Amadeo is practising on the foosball table all alone in a scene that could have been repeated on any day over the last ten years. "So, anyone want a game?" he asks hopefully. But there are no takers. There never are. The villagers have grown tired of Amadeo showing off his skills on the foosball table. "Er, anyone at all? I'll let you have a two goal start. No one? No one at all?"

Then the café door opens. A confident and attractive young woman enters and picks up a menu. It is Lara. Heads subtly turn to admire her elegance. The Guv'nor stands to attention behind the counter.

"I see that you still serve thirteen different types of chips. Can't believe that second Michelin star remains elusive," she adds witheringly. She scans the "specials" board advertising: "Small chips, regular chips, large chips, XL chips, XXL chips, Elvis circa-1976 chips, XXXL chips, supersized chips, super-supersized chips, Maradona super-super-supersized chips, God-size portion. All orders come with a free side of chips."

"Hmmm…" Lara wonders aloud, "Why chalk the so-called specials on a blackboard when they've never changed in anyone's lifetime? And what's special about them?"

"Every order comes with a free extra side of chips," proclaims the Guv'nor proudly.

"Could you please make me something with vegetables in it? A salad?"

"Dainty chips portion for the lady!" shouts the Guv'nor in the direction of the kitchen, where Chester is swatting flies with his spatula.

"I don't want chips!" says Lara firmly.

"But they're a vegetable," pleads the Guv'nor.

"Not really, they're a tuberous starchy carbohydrate."

"Eh?" is the Guvnor's response.

"Can you just boil some? That'll be healthier. Or do something a bit more creative?"

"Sorry, we only do chips. Chips is all you can do with a potato."

"You say 'potato', I say 'rosti'," says Lara.

"Eh?" repeats the Guv'nor.

"Or raclette, dauphinoise, tortilla, duchess," she adds.

"Eh, eh, eh and eh?" responds the Guv'nor, before adding with the enthusiasm of someone who has just had an unexpected brainwave, "I can serve you prawn cocktail."

"Really? Why didn't you say so earlier? That'll be great. Thank you. One prawn cocktail, please."

There is a very slight pause. "There you go," beams the Guv'nor with an accompanying look of problem-very-much-fixed.

"Of course," says Lara, "you're referring to crisps. Well, at least we discovered a second - if equally unhealthy - use for a potato. In that case," she adds, "I'll have anything that comes with vegetables. Even if that means having a plate of ketchup."

The Guv'nor disappears into the kitchen, presumably to read the labels on his jars of relish.

Amadeo has followed this exchange and now realises he is staring at Lara. His face flushes with embarrassment. "Wow, you look… fantastic," he greets her, hoping he has complimented not annoyed her with his comment.

"Thank you, Amadeo, but I'm a fully signed-up feminist now. Women will be ruling the world within the next few years. And when we become your overlords we will be standing over your souls - though men will probably still be trying to look up our skirts when we do."

Amadeo laughs nervously. "You're so witty, Lara," he stammers, again hoping he has complimented rather than patronised her. He suspects the latter.

Lara smiles. "We need to have a talk, Amadeo."

"Oh no, this sounds ominous," he thinks. "Am I like a manager about to receive a vote of confidence from the board?"

They find a quiet table, which is not difficult in the café these days - trade has not been good. "There's something I need to tell you," she says.

"What?" asks Amadeo, not enjoying his current feelings one little bit. "Sorry about my last remark sounding patronising. You know I support feminism too, right?"

"I know, Amadeo. You're a responsible penis owner. But it's not the threat to the patriarchy that I want to discuss. This is a lot more personal."

"Oh no," is all Amadeo can muster. A small sigh leaks out as he adopts the brace position for the obvious bad news heading for his direction.

"I'm leaving the village, Amadeo," Lara announces.

"But you'll be back by Saturday, right? I've got my foosball knock-out tournament first round game then here in the café," Amadeo says brightly, aware himself that he is probably exhibiting the classic signs of being in denial.

"I'm going away permanently, Amadeo."

"What! Where?" The blood is visibly draining away from his face.

"To the big city, to attend art college. This is my ticket to my dreams. I want to see life and paint it. I want to capture life with all the colours of the world, not just the same two or three colours I see here every day."

Amadeo wants to reply. But his mouth is suddenly incapable of moving.

"I'm sorry, Amadeo. I've shocked you. So what have you been up to?"

"Me? Loads of things. Let me think, where to start. Well, there's the café and I've been practising my foosball skills. Plus there's being here at the café and developing my new overhead bounce wall pass technique. Then there's the café, and on top of that I've been practising another foosball play involving an overhead triple axel kick. Did I mention the café and foosball?"

"Yes Amadeo, you did. Every time I see you," sighs Lara.

"You need to grow, Amadeo. Up and quickly. Goodbye, Amadeo."

She kisses him. An electric fission of energy fibrillates his body as a consequence.

"Sorry, salad's off," says the Guv'nor, who has returned empty-handed from the kitchen. "But we do have thirteen different types of special today."

Lara corrects him: "I think you mean you have thirteen different sorts of chips."

At this point her brother Chester appears through the kitchen door, his spectacles steamed up. "No need for alarm, Guv'nor, but where do we keep the fire extinguisher?"

Chester and the Guv'nor quickly disappear into the kitchen. A few moments later the Guv'nor reappears to announce: "Bad news: chips are off." There is a detectable groan of disappointment amongst the café regulars. "But there is some good menu news," he continues, "we now have lots of smoky bacon, smoky cheese and smoked fish. Maybe I could interest madam in some smoked potatoes?" he asks Lara hopefully.

Before Lara has a chance to decline, a terrifyingly loud sound from outside snatches everyone's attention.

KRRAAWWWWOOORRRRAAAKKK!!!!!!!

"What the…?" roars the Guv'nor, a huge mechanical crash rendering the final word of his exclamation inaudible.

The same sound suddenly thunders again. Only this time, even louder.

"It sounds like the sky is cracking into two!" says Lara.

Rushing out of the café and onto the village green, petrified staff and customers are greeted by a colourful sky lit by either pyrotechnics or artillery fire - no-one is quite sure yet which. "Is it Armageddon?" asks a startled village policeman. Parish priest Father Dick Dawkins is not sure. But Moxey is confident enough to make a prediction. "Definitely Armageddon," he confirms.

"It's only Armageddon if God's using four helicopters instead of horsemen," says Lara. "Well, even angels need to get with the technology of the times," replies Amadeo. "I fear this is no angel," says Lara ominously.

Laser lights coruscate. The deep roar of a helicopter, breaking away from its three outriding choppers, descends onto the village green. Out steps a bulky, flashily-dressed individual, puffing on an ostentatious cigar. Approaching a quickly erected podium, he flashes a sparkly smile revealing several gold fillings. News crews, obviously tipped off in advance, huddle beneath the microphone stand. Lara recognises him. "That's the Agent - formerly known as Mr. Fixer and, frequently, as the Accused."

Speakers have been hastily installed throughout the village green, and the Agent's amplified voice booms out with an echoing menace: "Hello proles... er, dear friends, of this decrepit... er, I mean... charming... village. You can trust me - I used to work at FIFA; surely that vouches for my stainless integrity. And I am here today to bring great news to your village. Like an Old Testament prophet I am descended here amongst you to make a great and mighty proclamation!"

"Get on with it, Moses!" heckles an unimpressed villager.

"Thank you, sir. I bet Moses never had to deal with hecklers. If he did there would only have been nine commandments not ten - he would have dispensed with that one about 'do not kill'. But I am here today to present to you the Universal Astro Dome! Smile reassuringly at crowd so they don't suspect they're being conned. Ignore that last bit - I wasn't supposed to read it off the autocue. For we are setting up a project that will attract tourists to this backwater... er... characterful village. And deliver lots of lovely lolly for everyone. Hence I give you the Astro Dome – or Asbo Dome if it's built around here by the look of these villagers... whoops, said that too close to the microphone. Now pay attention, villagers, for this is the brainchild of a man raised amongst you in this outdated... umm... historic village. That's right, he used to be one of your own."

Dazzling starbursts cascade from the newly bright purple sky.

"This time it might actually be Armageddon," whispers Amadeo.

As the light show and pyrotechnics fade into the starlit sky, a muscular figure standing in backlit silhouette is revealed, awaiting the settled silence of his audience. He stands loftily above the villagers on an elevated platform, lifting his hands slowly outwards in a stance reminiscent of Christ the Redeemer overlooking Rio de Janeiro. Looking down on his people, he is dressed like a superhero. His inadequately sized red and black designer outfit struggles to contain the enormous muscles that are deliberately emphasised by his wardrobe choice. He looks like a cross between an action hero, cage fighter and a Batman collectible.

But it is the Agent who speaks next, addressing the shell-shocked crowd from the podium, "He may be an international superstar now, a global brand, but he was just a kid when I signed him up. We knew then, playing for Albion Rovers Second Eleven that he should be known henceforth as an acronym. I give you FLASH: Football Legend And Soccer Hero. He earns more money in one second than most of you earn in a year - assuming any of you have jobs. This button here that I've just pressed is the one that mutes the microphone, right?"

Amadeo and Lara stand transfixed in front of several million pounds of PR extravaganza and razzmatazz, their consternation matched by the expression on the faces of the other villagers. Before them stands none other than Flash - the former village bully, tormentor of Amadeo's youth. Flash approaches the newly popped-up podium posturing like a bodybuilder. Two women faint when they recognise him as an international megastar. "Why is it impossible for women to remain upright in my presence?" he muses aloud. As he climbs several steps to the stage a deafening rock anthem proclaims that Flash is master of the universe. The music subsides when he approaches a cluster of microphones and begins delivering his speech in a portentous tone.

"Now a news Flash! Ha, that's so clever. News Flash. Genius. Really I am."

"Get on with it," shouts another brave heckler. Flash doesn't consider this interruption worthy of raising an eyebrow let alone his voice, but seconds later an audible "ouuuchhh!" is heard from the place in the crowd where the heckle originated - one of Flash's henchmen, intolerant of any opposition towards his megalomaniac master, has got to work on any dissenters. Flash continues, this time without anyone daring to interrupt him: "My village will be sacrificed in order for a greater, bolder, superior, nobler creation to come into being. That's right, my village will be transformed into a tribute to the noblest of sports: the largest, greatest and most globally dominant of all sports."

"Wow, at last - we're getting a beach volleyball stadium!" exclaims Chester loudly. And then rather wishes he hadn't. Rightly concluding he should try to say something better, he shouts: "Hey, Bigshot, why do you keep referring to it as 'MY village'?"

"That's simple: because it's a village and it's mine. Furthermore the biggest and greatest football stadium on the planet will be built here. Where currently I only see a dreary, boring backwater, I will transform this emptiness into greatness. Next to the stadium will be a football research area built to improve the science behind football. Plus a museum dedicated to the all-time footballing greats: me, Pele, Cruyff, Messi, Ronaldo and Emile Heskey."

This is too much for Lara: "No you will not. This is an outage," she screams at Flash. "Have you ever heard of the concept of planning permission? None of you supervillains, with your monstrous plans and underground criminal liars, ever consider the planning regulations." Their bravery buoyed by Lara's fearless dissent, several other villagers shout their objection to Flash's plans.

"Interesting responses. I think you'll find that the paperwork is all in order. I own this village, and currently you are all trespassing. That is all." And Flash folds his arms, like a man who has just made a checkmate move and is enjoying watching his opponent's hopeless quest to discover a square where the king can escape.

"That's impossible. There's no way the mayor will allow it to happen," shouts a hopeful villager.

But her comment is drowned out by the loud blades of yet another helicopter. Turning their heads towards the roof of the town hall, most villagers are in time to see their mayor running with head ducked down and jumping into a waiting helicopter - one of the choppers that had escorted Flash's grand descent. It is clearly the sight of someone wanting to make a quick exit. Several banknotes float free from hastily packed and bulging suitcases as he throws them into the cockpit.

"Surely not! The mayor has sold the village, and sold us all out too!" groans a forlorn local.

"Don't forget to give me a good seller's rating on an online auction site!" shouts the mayor as his farewell words to the village.

"It's almost as if politicians can't be trusted. I simply cannot believe that a politician has engaged in something that would give him a bad reputation. I don't think that's ever happened before," remarks one of the villagers to the others still assembled on the green.

But the interlude to discuss corruption and politics is brief. For now the village has an even more immediate problem to deal with. A dark shadow is looming over its future - literally - in the shape of a swinging wrecking ball.

"This won't take long, as I'm sure all you villagers are anxious to get back to your dreary lives. Oh yes, but there's one more thing," continues Flash from the podium, "I was supposed to give advance notice about your café being destroyed. But I was too busy, out and about being great and famous to get around to it. So it's last orders at the café… right about now!"

With those baleful words still hanging in the air, a crane swings its wrecking ball through the café window. Moxey, Spencer and the Emo Kid dive for cover. Chester, seemingly unaware of the Newtonian laws of physics, bravely runs towards the huge spherical object in an attempt to divert it from customers, but misses it completely, the ball slipping straight through his hands but luckily avoiding a collision with anyone else. Even the incredible strength of the Guv'nor cannot neutralise the power of the wrecking ball's destructive arc.

The bespectacled, rotund Chester notices Gill Etre, the much-respected local lady remarkably unbothered by her extensive facial hair, walking past the village café just as the wrecking ball is being drawn back, primed for another crashing destructive release. Determined to be a hero, Chester makes a split decision to hurl himself towards Gill, attempting to push her out of harm's way. Unfortunately, he completely misses his intended target again. Fortunately so does the wrecking ball. Chester fumbles for his glasses on the ground, picks them up, and promptly drops them.

With the café now missing at least three walls, a giant metal claw reaches into the rubble where the café had stood only a few seconds earlier. Its metallic jaw clasps the foosball table and lifts it up and away, disappearing like a dinosaur with struggling prey in its mouth. Amadeo and Lara hear the unmistakably evil laugh of Flash, a man naturally devoid of doubt - and compassion. "I'll be taking the table. I think, after all these years, it may soon be time for a re-match."

Lara can take no more. She sprints towards Flash. "No, Lara - be careful. He's a megalomaniac," shouts Amadeo in warning. "I'll save her," yells Chester, and like a knight of old determined to save a damsel, the porky protector hurls himself at Flash - only to miss completely. "Think I might need to get new glasses," he concludes wistfully.

"All this senseless destruction. Our brave village has stood for hundreds of years. How could you do this?" Lara shouts accusingly at Flash.

Amadeo warns Lara again: "He doesn't even know who we are, Lara."

"Oh, I will always remember you two. The duo who dared to beat me," Flash replies.

"What? You've doing all this because you lost a game of table football as a child," asks Lara with disbelief.

"I do not lose. I never lose. If I lose, there are consequences. Bigger consequences than your small minds are capable of comprehending," Flash replies ominously.

"So you really are causing all this destruction because of a foosball match?" asks Lara again.

"You think I care about losing at a child's football game… no, wait, actually, that's exactly what it is. Ten years in therapy without a breakthrough, then today ha, ha, ha, ha I'm so brilliant at sarcasm too."

"And humility," adds Lara.

"Yes that's true. I am genuinely brilliant at humility. Really. I am. Number one."

"Flash, listen," begins Lara earnestly, trying hard to regulate her voice and reduce her visible anger levels. But inside she still just wants to scream at Flash as he appears to be the same immature, spoilt bully he was all those years previously - only now occupying a fully grown adult's body. And a dangerous position of power and wealth.

"Flash, listen to someone else for once."

"Like Gary Lineker, I'm all ears," he replies.

The urge to put her arms around his neck and shake him is as great as ever, but she has to focus on staying composed and coherent. "What you're doing is wrong. Wrong on so many levels. This is our village where people live and work. Our community. Our space. This village green is where you learnt to play football. You cannot just bulldoze it for some soulless new stadium."

"You're wrong," counteracts Flash. "It's MY village, not yours, and I can bulldoze any part I like. Indeed, if you care to look around, you can maybe… oh yes, there's one… spot a bulldozer!"

Sure enough, huge yellow bulldozers are approaching the village from a hillside, like the unstoppable tanks of an invading army.

"Goodbye - oh, just to clarify, that 'goodbye' was to the village, not you. Now, I'm due back on my helicopter - I don't want to hang around here for too long, this place is so flat nowadays - especially after my bulldozers arrive. Ha, I really don't think anyone has been as witty as me before. So why don't you and I pop back to my palace for a spot of dinner. Come on, you know you want to dine with a demi-God."

"You're not a demi-God, you're a psychotic braggart and a stupid…" Lara's impassioned choice of noun is obliterated by the rotating helicopter blades. "You're right. I'm much more of a full-on God figure, aren't I, not a demi-God. I'm far too modest, always selling myself short." Flash offers those words, devoid of irony, as his athletic muscular frame clambers up the steps into his personal helicopter.

Suddenly Flash grabs Lara. "Hey, let go of me!" But it is too late. Caught off-guard, her protests go unheeded. Lara is swooped up into the helicopter by Flash's muscular arms. "You do realise there's a crucial difference between a date and an abduction?" she shouts.

6

Separated by the chaos of crashing masonry and destruction around them, Amadeo has become separated from Lara - a situation that now threatens to become permanent with her notion of going to the city to study art. Forlornly, he wanders the outskirts of the village, resembling a refugee from a war already lost.

His knees suddenly twist and he sinks to the ground. Tears take him by surprise. Unnoticed in his distressed state, a rod from the foosball table lies abandoned on the ground nearby - broken off by the wrecking ball and propelled to its current resting place. A tear falls right onto the face of the Stripes' central forward Skip. The unanimated toy footballer lies motionless, like a slain soldier, at the side of the road. Amadeo now sobs openly, distraught at the triple loss of the café, foosball table and Lara. Another tear sprinkles the toy footballer spatchcocked on a broken steel rod. Laying on his back, Skip swivels himself anti-clockwise, unscrewing himself from his restraining metal rod in the process.

Unsteady at first, the miniature footballer starts to move. Skip attempts to stand up, swaying like a drunken man, but promptly topples over - like a striker looking for an optimistic penalty. He tries again, with the same result. Amadeo notices something moving, but dismisses it as an apparition caused by his distressed emotional state.

"Hey, Amadeo?" shouts Skip.

Amadeo, unaccustomed to having real two-way conversations with actual speaking toy footballers, understandably ignores him.

"Oi, Amadeo - down here!" But Skip's presence remains unacknowledged. Amadeo is very busy feeling sorry for himself right now and wants the world to know the "Do Not Disturb" sign is up.

"Hey Amadeo! Amadeo!? Well, that's just rude. Particularly after all the goals I've scored for you," shouts Skip. A remark loaded with such raw controversy snaps Amadeo back into the world. He hinges forward.

"Goals you scored for me? It was my handiwork - my wrist skills that scored them all," he retorts.

"Nonsense, it was my positional play, gambling where to go in the area, my sharpness in front of goal…"

"Just a minute…" Amadeo pauses, "I'm not thinking straight am I?"

"See… I knew you'd realise that I'm the goal scorer, the architect of the goals. Yeah, you helped a bit, sure, a good manager is important, but I deserve the credit for scoring all those net-bound beauties, dominating the box," continues Skip.

"I'm not thinking straight because I'm currently having a conversation with a tiny lump of lead," Amadeo concludes.

"Lump of lead? That's not very nice. I've still got my pace, you know."

36

"No you haven't."

"I'm fitter than a butcher's dog that works out."

"No you're not."

Skip has an immediate comeback. "Well I'm not the one sitting in a pool of my own tears feeling sorry for myself. Why the long face - did some girl show you the red card?"

"Yeah," admits Amadeo, more forlornly than Skip was expecting.

Skip isn't expecting to be a counsellor so soon after his liberation from being a footballer stuck to a pole, but he decides to do his best and counsels away: "So, let her go. She'd only be a distraction for the team anyway. Remember we're a team. You don't need a girl. How many of the Beatles' best songs did Yoko write? Girls are alright, don't get me wrong, but you wouldn't want to live with one. I saw a female foosball player once, boss - she was OK but being a foosball player meant she couldn't open her legs."

"I don't think I want to hear this, Skip."

"She was great because no one was ever going to nutmeg her."

"Oh… I see," says a relieved Amadeo.

"But girls distract the team, boss, and we can't have that."

"The reason you say things like that is because your brain - and heart - are literally made out of lead."

"That's as maybe. But we're a team. The Stripes. A team that has just gone three thousand five hundred and twenty-one games unbeaten. I think you can call that a run."

You could also call his comment other things. Like insensitive. Amadeo dabs at his tears and stands up, brushing dust from his legs. "Ok, get a grip, I probably just got a glancing blow to the head from falling debris when Flash's thugs demolished the café. That's it - I've got concussion. That's why I'm currently conversing with a lead-brained two-inch high chauvinist. I'm concussed, that's all. Hold up some fingers, Skip, and I'll count them. Oh, that's actually quite rude."

"Well, you deserve it if you don't respect the team. Three

thousand, five hundred and twenty-two games unbeaten."

"It's gone up one, you just said…"

"Whatever."

Amadeo slumps back down to the dusty ground. "We're all in the gutter, but some of us are looking up at the Stripes." He lets out a deep sigh. "I've lost everything."

"You haven't lost the team," says Skip consolingly.

"This cannot be happening. No. It's really happening. That's the denial stage over quickly."

"No, boss," begins Skip, his tone rising towards a crescendo. "So we've conceded early on. But we dig in and grind out a result."

"What are you talking about? I've wasted my entire life playing foosball. And now I've lost everything I ever had. Which, if we're being analytical, wasn't that much. And that's my fault too." "You're talking like a loser, that's what you're talking like," says Skip. "What are you talking about, Amadeo? We never lose. We can still win, but only as a team. This is our half-time pep talk and we need the hair-dryer treatment."

But Skip's message does not appear to be getting through to Amadeo.

"I'm a total loser. I've lost the whole lot: the foosball table, the café, Lara and here I am talking to a toy like it's a normal thing to do. Probably best not to mention this to anyone."

"I'm not just a toy. Or lump of lead. Or a loser," begins Skip, his voice angling upwards into a thunderous proclamation. "I am a foosball player. The captain of the best foosball team on the planet. Three thousand five hundred and twenty-three games unbeaten."

"It's gone up again."

"Shut up. And YOU! YOU are the undefeated champion of the world. Don't you remember that game against Flash when you were kids? You were 3-nil down and what happened? 4-3 up! He laughed at you and you thrashed him. Remember how he laughed at you?"

Amadeo mocks Flash's laugh: "Ha ha ha. Not a great evil laugh, I grant you."

"His evil laugh was very much a work in progress. He sounded like an asthmatic hyena." Skip impersonates Flash's pathetic evil laugh. "Yeah - that's it," enthuses Amadeo.

"He laughed like a badly constipated Mutley!"

"And his dumb henchmen bully friends with their high-pitched voices laughed like this: 'Ho ho ho ho' - like Santa on helium."

Skip and Amadeo both laugh. A bonding laugh.

"Remember," Skip reminisces, "We were 3-nil down against Flash and what happened? 4-3! It's about the team. No-one else. Let's get the team back together. Let's go find the boys. The team's all we need."

Yet instead of appearing elated, Amadeo looks sad again, close to tears. "The team can't bring Lara back."

"Forget Lara," counsels Skip. "She held up the substitution board, and your number was on it. She's replaced you for Flash. It's the team that matters now. As a team we fear no-one. Not Flash. Not his rubbish evil laugh… Ho ho…"

But Skip's efforts are not working. Amadeo is still looking miserable now he has remembered Lara.

Skip tries again. "We win as a team. 3-nil down, 4-3 up."

Amadeo stands up and starts walking. Instinctively Skip follows. "Hey, slow down - I've only got little legs, remember." Amadeo picks up Skip who climbs onto his shoulder, enabling his captain to talk straight into his ear. "It's all about the team." "The team," repeats Amadeo.

"Not the village," says Skip.

"Not the village," echoes Amadeo.

"Not the café." "Not the café." "Not Lara." "Not Lara."

There is a pause, then Amadeo declares: "I need Lara."

"Yeah, should have predicted you'd say that. And of course you'll win Lara back," Skip adds encouragingly, "if we get the team back first. Think of Lara as your World Cup." There is a pause while Amadeo dreams of picking up Lara, as she stands with her arms on hips, and lifting her to the adulation of a stadium crowd. "Literally a trophy girlfriend!" quips Skip. "I don't think Lara would like you describing her like that. She's so… great and… er… really great."

"Yeah. Promise me you'll never write romantic poetry."

Suddenly Amadeo looks more determined. Seizing upon his new mood, Skip issues a battle cry: "Let's go and pick a team for Saturday." "Yeah. The boys. But where are they?"

"Flash has taken them."

"Where?" "Don't know," says Skip.

"There are rumours most of them have ended up on the rubbish heap."

"What? Joined West Ham?"

"No, literally on the rubbish heap."

"Millwall?"

"No, on an actual, real-life rubbish dump."

"Of course," muses Amadeo, "Flash's workmen would have taken all the debris and rubble from demolishing the café to the rubbish dump. That's where the foosball table must be."

"Then let's go to the dump," says Skip firmly.

7

A large municipal sign announces they are at the rubbish dump: "Toxic Dump (twinned with Swindon)". Signs are definitely important in this environment - there are signs announcing all sorts of dangers: that hardhats must be worn, lorries are reversing, dangerous substances must be contained, and that it has now been 6 days since a major accident occurred on the site. Suddenly there is a scream from inside the compound. Minutes later a workman climbs up a ladder and changes the sign from "6 days" to "0 days".

Bulldozers are pushing piles of rubbish. Between two teetering garbage piles a miniature head pops out of a discarded drinks carton. The tiny head belongs a tiny foosballer. Named Loco by Amadeo, he is bedecked in the same green and yellow striped shirt as Skip. He moves uneasily. Lying on his back and struggling to stand up, he flounders like an upturned tortoise. "Wow, man, my head! That must have been some industrial sized doofer I sparked up last night," he remarks, while combing his black dreadlocks with his fingers. "If my headspace is a party I really don't like what the DJ's currently spinning."

Next to him - at equally spaced intervals in a straight line - are his teammates: big-haired playmaker Rico and Korean midfielder Psy Kick. They are all connected to a pole, resembling a footballer kebab. Which explains why Loco couldn't stand-up. Yet he is unaccustomed to lying on his back.

"My head is spinning, man," announces Loco. "Yeah, what a night," agrees Rico. "Rico remembers George Best having to go home early because he couldn't keep up."

Then Loco suddenly notices something. "Hey, where's the rest of the team?" Aware that the three Stripes players have somehow broken away from their team, and feeling disorientated, Rico, Psy Kick and Loco jump to their feet and run. Unfortunately, running in different directions while connected to a pole means they topple over in an undignified heap. "Penalty, ref? Surely!" pleads Rico hopefully, "sorry, old habits die hard."

"Yeah, we made a rod for our own back there, guys," adds Loco. "We so need to chill out more." Korean midfielder Psy Kick raises his hand to indicate silence is needed. Pensively, after several seconds of contemplation, he announces: "We appear to be connected to a pole."

"Wow, Psy Kick is, like his names implies, psychic. Although cynics would point out that before he made that startling observation, we have all spent our entire lives connected to a poll. After all, we are the vital midfield combo in a foosball team," says Rico sarcastically.

"Our connection as a single team entity has been broken, man," Loco adds.

"Rico would like to quote an ancient proverb for Loco: 'Give the new age claptrap a rest, you daft hippie.' Thank you - that concludes the proverb."

"I mean our connection has literally been broken. You need to open your eyes, guys. Our pole has been snapped off. We are no longer in the bar, or on the foosball table. Or with our teammates!"

The three foosballers, attached together all their lives by a steel pole, are now suddenly free. But they are also on their own.

"So where are the others, man?" ponders Loco.

"Rico always expected to leave his teammates, but because of a big money transfer to one of the world's best sides - not this way."

Loco starts to chant his Buddhist mantra, "OOmmmmmm", something he does regularly to calm himself down. Ironically, this always has the effect of not calming down his teammates. "Shut up!" demands Rico, "Rico cannot stand this annoying new-age chanting. Rico's mind and body are a perfectly co-ordinated machine and must not be exposed to stress." Loco's chanting increases in volume. "Right, that's it, don't make me come over there and shut you up in person. Right, Rico is coming to shut you up. Rico is getting nearer… Rico is making a fist… this is your last chance… Rico has now arrived in your face to shut you up in person… er… what's happened? Rico is very confused."

Rico has good reason to be confused. After being restrained by a pole all his life, he now appears to have free movement. The screws that held him in place snapped when the demolition crew dragged the foosball table out of the café in the jaws of a crane. He forgets that he is about to hit the chanting Loco.

"Hey, Loco, Psy Kick! Look! Look!! Rico is free. If Rico was the team's leading scorer tied to a pole, imagine what Rico can accomplish now!"

"I am always free too. The mind can never be imprisoned without the permission of its owner," says Loco philosophically, performing a calming breathing ritual. "Even on my pole, I always felt free. Now my body as well as my mind is free. It just goes to show, dudes, free your mind and your booty will follow."

"This is incredible. Rico can move, walk, run. Rico can actually dance without a pole. Look, Rico can move without needing Amadeo," declares Rico.

"Guys. Look. We appear to have become unattached from our steel rod," adds Psy Kick.

"That's lad is Psy Kick," says Rico.

Elsewhere in the rubbish dump Amadeo and Skip are fruitlessly searching for their teammates. "On my head, son," announces Amadeo to Skip. "What? We haven't got a ball."

"No," says Amadeo, "I mean literally get on my head. That way we can have a higher vantage point. You can scan the horizon - like a meerkat. Simples."

Amadeo picks Skip up and places him on his head.

"Nothing. Can't see them. They could be anywhere," sighs Skip, before adding, "how much stuff do you humans reject? This is ridiculous. You just bury this stuff? That empty bottle down there could be recycled."

Amadeo bends down carefully so as not to dislodge Skip, and picks up the bottle. "Put that to your eye," he suggests. "We can use it as an improvised telescope." Amadeo helps hold it to Skip's right eye.

"Nothing."

"Scan a few degrees to the left," Amadeo tells him.

"Still nothing."

"Try moving a bit more to the left."

"No, still nothing… Oh wow… Rico is doing what he always wanted to do…"

"What?" asks Amadeo impatiently.

"He's choreographing his goal celebration," says Skip.

"Yes, I suppose that was a bit tricky when he was connected to a metal pole," agrees Amadeo.

"Can humans dance around a pole?" asks Skip

"Er…"

"I suppose not," says Skip. "I can't imagine Lara dancing around a pole, can you Amadeo?"

"I'm not thinking about that right now… OK, maybe for a bit… the point is some people think it's demeaning if… JUST A MINUTE!"

"What?!" asks a suddenly startled Skip.

"You've seen Rico?" asks Amadeo, his voice rising with excitement.

Skip says casually, "Yeah, he's over there. With Loco and Psy Kick."

"You didn't think it important to mention it?"

The next moment, Skip and Amadeo run towards their teammates for an emotional reunion.

"Loco, Rico, Psy Kick! It's so good to see you guys again,"

says Skip - not quite sure how to hug another man. He tries a visibly awkward hug with Loco. Loco knows how to hug properly though, and Skip becomes agitated when Loco opts not to release him for several seconds. Amadeo, meanwhile, finds hugging even more awkward than Skip - principally because his fellow huggers are only a few centimetres tall.

"Yeah, it's good to see you too, Skip. But it must be really good for you to see Rico again, the team's only natural goalscorer."

"What?" snaps Skip. "I contribute just as many goals as you, and I play in midfield."

"Clearly you are concussed. Rico scores all the goals. And it's not easy when there's poor service from midfield. And the captain never passes."

"Never passes?" Skip is becoming outraged.

"Yeah," continues Rico, "you're like an old lady driver - you never pass."

Skip, his face now glowing an incandescent orange colour, blusters, "If I passed to you, you'd lose it."

"Rico chooses not to listen to such nonsense. Rico is above this. Rico is the top goalscorer."

"Really? You're so irritating you must have been a wasp in a previous life."

"My genius is weighed down by the burden of playing with water carriers like you."

"Muzzle it, brillo head!" snarls Skip.

This is too much for Rico, prompting him to announce - unwisely given he has clearly forgotten his new rod-free status, "That's it. I'm going to come over there now and break your head."

"OK, come on then," taunts Skip, "bring it on. If you think you're hard enough."

Suddenly aware that he now has a major problem - specifically that there is no longer a bar holding him and Skip apart - Rico stands transfixed.

Psy Kick breaks the silence. "Rico is reluctant to fight now that he can."

Instead, Rico chooses, hands on hips, to deliver what he thinks are home truths to Skip: "You are not this team's leading scorer. Rico is. Rico is the most accurate finisher in this team. Rico always hits the target."

"If you threw a stone off the end of a pier, you'd still miss the sea," Skip retorts.

Loco has had enough of the squabbling. He issues a directive to his teammates. "Guys, calm down. Take some chill pills, yeah? This is bad football karma. We're a team. And we need to be one. Together as a whole. We complete the team, and the team completes us. Without the team I'd be like a Loco without a motive. And a Loco needs a motive to become a Locomotive, especially if I have to carry passengers."

"That's true," concedes Rico.

"I agree," concurs Skip

"We need to be one with the universe too," adds Loco. "Then, when we find our team we will be eleven, plus one with the universe, which makes twelve - so we'll have to bench the universe and make it a sub."

"Not sure I agree with that bit," says Skip.

Amadeo decides to step in carefully. Quite literally. As he has to be careful not to tread on the tiny foosballers. "You guys must realise Loco is right."

"Not necessarily. Rico knows Loco talks so much nonsense."

Loco continues: "In football it is important to express oneself."

"And I'm expressing myself now: you're a pillock, Loco," says Skip.

"Your tears are seagulls following the sardines of regret caught by the trawler of hope," remarks Loco somewhat mystifyingly.

"You're an idiot," concludes Rico.

"We can all be idiots, yet a man too," says Loco.

"I am not a man, I am Rico."

"That's right, you're not a man. You're a hairstyle with a prat attached," observes Skip.

Loco steps in again: "Calm down, guys. Everyone recite their favourite peace mantra and set their SatNav for destination cosmic chill-out."

"Rico should not be insulted in this way."

"You're right," agrees Skip, "We should make much more of an effort."

The bickering seems set to continue until suddenly a Scottish voice booms out: "You lot are even more pathetic than I remembered. And I remember you being very, very pathetic." The voice belongs to Gregor, captain and mainstay of the Clarets' defence, perennial opponents of the Stripes on the foosball table.

"Gregor?" says a surprised Skip.

"It's Gregor," announces Rico.

"Gregor. You're here?" asks Amadeo.

Gregor steps out from behind the heel of a discarded ladies' shoe.

Psy Kick remarks: "Gregor is here everyone."

Skip greets his opposing captain: "You look pathetic… I mean… pretty in pink, Gregor."

In his deep Glaswegian brogue, Gregor replies: "Firstly, it is claret not pink, as you well know. And besides, if I'm so pathetic how come my team always beats yours?"

47

"You don't always beat us. In fact, you never beat us," Skip counters.

"You're right, sometimes we just humiliate you instead."

Needless to say, Skip does not accept Gregor's point. "Really? How many games have you won? Let's work it out… carry 6… add 8… carry 7… oh yeah. I've worked out the answer now… NONE!"

Gregor picks up the pole that until only a few moments ago had restrained him and his fellow Clarets and waves it threateningly at the Stripes players. "I'll reattach you lot to your poles permanently - by impaling you!"

Gregor had expected the Stripes to look worried, but not quite as worried as they suddenly appear, for at that very moment an expression of pure terror appears on their faces. "I'm not really going to do it - you don't have to look THAT frightened," says Gregor, before adding nervously, "there's something behind me, isn't there?"

Judging from the Stripes' collective look of horror, their faces bleached by fear, there is indeed something behind Gregor that they can see - and he cannot.

"Well, talk to me. What's the matter? Rat got your tongue?" asks Gregor, not daring to look over his shoulder.

"Move very slowly, Gregor," Skip whispers. He would like to add "you normally do", but this is an inappropriate time for banter. "If you have to turn round, and I advise you not to, may I also suggest that screaming would be appropriate?"

But Gregor cannot resist satisfying his curiosity by turning around. And just as quickly he wishes he hadn't. First he sees the monster's teeth, two sharp protruding fangs both as big as he is. Surrounding the teeth is an enormous salivating mouth, and around the mouth is lots of dirty fur. It's a rat the size of a small car.

"RUUNNNN!!!!!!!" scream the tiny foosball players in unison.

The rat charges after them, drooling and salivating with the expectancy of his upcoming meal. The foosballers are running as fast as their tiny leaden feet will allow, but the rat scurries towards them, its long tail swishing in sinister fashion. Rico trips and falls. "Leave Rico to be, go on and save yourselves. Console yourself with the memory that there will be one piece of this rubbish tip that will be forever Rico."

"Come on, drama queen," says Skip picking him up.

"Rico objects to that description - Rico is not a drama queen. Hey, be careful with the hair."

Spotting an upturned sofa, Skip dives for cover. "What? So I dived. It happens," he says.

The other foosball players join him, hiding behind the discarded sofa.

"Where's the rat?! Have we lost them?" whispers Gregor.

"There are two giant eyes staring at us. The creature also has a long thin tail and is very terrifying. With sharp teeth. Psy Kick concludes we have not lost the rat."

"Yiikkkkessss! Run! Save yourselves!" yells Skip.

"The rat is definitely still here," Psy Kick confirms - unnecessarily.

"AARRRRGGHH!!! RUN!!!!"

The foosballers flee once more, pursued by the rat gnashing its razor-sharp teeth with every stride. Trailing behind, Rico's extravagant coiffure is not aerodynamically efficient and his huge hair soon slows him down. Twice the rat gets close enough to snap at his locks. "Oi, mind the hair, Rico does not want a dodgy barnet!"

"This is horrible," pants Loco as he runs. "The rat never behaved like this in *The Wind in the Willows*."

"Rico can't believe footballers are going to die like this. Bitten to death with fearsome fangs. And Luis Suarez isn't even here."

"Look, a house!" yells Skip. "Let's try and get inside - we're small enough to get through the door, but the rat won't be able to get in!" A panting Skip leads his men, and Gregor, into an abandoned wooden doll's house. "Men, did we all make it? Loco and Psy Kick you're here? Thank God. One of the Pinks is here too."

"Clarets!" responds Gregor impatiently.

"Where's Rico?" asks Skip

No one has seen Rico.

"Poor Rico. Why did we fight? He's my teammate. Now I feel worthless." Skip struggles for words through emotional sniffs. "We are all worthless and he was, er, worthful."

"See, footballers can be profound not shallow," adds Loco. "Hmm... I'll get that put on a new tattoo."

"Poor Rico is gone. And he scored all the goals you know," mutters Skip, on the edge of tears.

"And he was so modest," adds Loco.

"Yeah he was a really modest, humble guy. A great guy. He really was," says Skip disconsolately, now openly crying. "And the Stripes' leading goal scorer."

There is a reflective pause while the foosballers remember their fallen colleague.

"Hey guys, check out some of the wigs and fuchsia dresses here. Rico's been in the wardrobe of this doll's house checking out this fab-u-lous gear!" It's the unmistakable voice of Rico.

"Why didn't we check for him in the closet? We ought to have guessed that's where he always is," says Skip, his tears suddenly turned to a mix of relief and anger.

"That rat is scary," announces Psy Kick profoundly.

"Of course it's scary. That's why I suggested screaming," says Skip.

A continuous loud knocking at the door begins. "Sorry, that's my heart beating. Still a bit scared of the rat," says Skip. Boom, boom. "OK, it's not just my heart - I think there's someone at the door."

"It'll be the rat," says Rico.

In fact, it is another visitor - and one who is much more welcome than the rat. "Amadeo?" asks Loco nervously.

Amadeo's giant face peers in through the doll's house door. "Guys, I've found you. Jump into this box. I'll carry my team."

"Makes a change from Rico always having to carry my team," quips Rico, to hardly unanimous agreement.

"Why you little…" Skip lunges towards Rico's neck.

"Violence is a negative expression," says Loco soothingly. Skip lowers his fists unused and holsters them back in his pockets.

Outside the rubbish dump is now eerily quiet. The rat has gone. "I see the rat has given up on your team - guess it recognises a sinking ship when it sees one," quips Gregor.

"If anyone knows about going down, it's you," Skip retorts. "How many relegations have the Pinks suffered?"

"It's Clarets!" snarls Gregor.

"Didn't deny the relegations, did you?" insists Skip.

Amadeo gives them both a "this isn't helping" look. As a consequence, Gregor tries introducing a more conciliatory mood. "Guys, we need to find the others - and that's both teams. Without an opposition you'll have no one to play against."

Loco speaks deliberately slowly, loading his comment with perceptiveness: "The Pinkman is right. We need to look not just for the rest of our team, but also for the Pinks."

"…Clarets," interjects Gregor, not for the first time.

"A lone wolf can only howl his appreciation for the wolf pack," adds Loco. "Only in unity will we have a future. Our pack needs to be flat."

"Loco is right - about from the last bit, obviously," says Amadeo, "we need to find the other Stripes and Clarets."

"Thank you," says Gregor. "You see, 'Clarets' isn't such a hard word to pronounce."

"All of you - instead of arguing we need to look for a bottle amongst all this rubbish," says Amedeo. Sifting through a nearby pile of discarded kitchen waste, Psy Kick soon finds one.

"Really, Loco is appalled at humans' inability to recycle. Such short-term obsolescence is blind to Mother Nature's tears."

Amadeo picks up the bottle and raises it to his eye, again using it as a makeshift telescope. "It worked last time, as a bottle enabled us to spot you. Wow! There's Jono and Stevie our fullbacks. And with him are some of the Clarets. And some more Stripes including Beville!"

"What about his twin brother?" asks Skip.

"Yes, they're both there: Beville and his twin brother Beville Beville."

"Let's go and join them," suggests Skip. Amadeo picks up Skip, Gregor, Rico, Loco and Psy Kick, puts them in his jacket pocket and carries them across the rubbish tip in the direction of the other foosballers. Loco peers out of Amadeo's pocket and remarks, "Wow, this place is such a dump."

A few moments later Amadeo has reached the others and the big reunion is under way. "Amadeo!" shouts Beville. "Great to see you guys, but we're still missing several players - anyone seen the others?" The moment of euphoria as the reunited Stripes and Clarets hug each other is suddenly over, the players' mood just as quickly turning to sadness as they begin to work out who is missing from each team.

But their roll-call is abruptly stopped by the intensity of two search beacons lighting up their faces. "Someone's looking for us! Quick, hide over here - behind these old boots!" orders Skip. "Oi! No one tells my team what to do!" snarls Gregor. "Quick, hide over here - behind these old boots."

"Quiet! Look, it's the Agent!" Amadeo whispers to the foosballers. "He's the guy who made the speech about destroying our village on behalf of Flash. He's slimy, smarmy and so crooked he has problems hanging pictures straight on his walls. He even had to resign from FIFA."

The Agent's voice is soon audible to the concealed foosballers. "Oi, you, what's your name? Oh, who cares what your name is…" The hiding Amadeo briefly fears that the Agent has spotted him and is directing the question at him. But, to his relief, the Agent is instead addressing his chauffeur and henchmen who are standing by his limo, its oversized vulgarity somehow emphasised by the dump with its heaps of discarded junk. "Round up any tiny toy footballers you see," barks the Agent. "Quickly, you know His Highness back at the palace is impatient." Three henchmen switch on their torches, scanning the dump for the foosballers. Amadeo immediately recognises them - they were in Young Flash's bully entourage all those years earlier when they tormented him in the village café. One of the henchmen accidentally steps on the train of the Agent's long and ostentatious coat. "Hey, mind the threads, cretin. This coat is made from the fur of at least three endangered species."

"Look, it's the others!" bursts out an elated Skip - slightly too loudly, as they are supposed to be hiding. "Ssshhh," hisses Amadeo, "Do you want the Agent and his henchmen to discover us?" Compliantly lowering his voice, Skip whispers, "It's the rest of the Stripes and Pinks. He's taking them."

The Agent barks at the three henchmen: "You three, what are you called again? You know what, I'm bored by my own question… pick up that foosball table and get it into the van, you useless sack of uselessness. His Flashness wants it - the Flash git - along with the players. Why His Arrogance wants these toys I really don't know, shows what a massive child he is. Then again we all knew that. And there's another player over there - look, with the green and yellow striped shirt, get him. Oi! There's another one over there too - another pink one."

"I think you'll find it's Claret!" calls Gregor from his hiding position.

"Ssshhhh!!!" everyone whispers in unison.

"Where?" continues Gregor, "I can't see another pink, I mean Claret. There aren't any more of our players... oh rude word, he means me, doesn't he?" He now regrets having just stood up.

Amadeo spots an empty shoe box on the rubbish heap and grabs it. He knows that Gregor will be captured by the Agent and delivered with the others to Flash, unless he takes immediate action. "Quick", says Amadeo urgently to the foosballers, "everyone jump into this box and put yourself in the brace position. This game just started to get a bit physical."

Clutching the box, Amadeo starts to sprint towards the empty car while the Agent and his minions are busy scanning the junkyard for the remaining foosball players. "Quick, let's get in and drive this thing out of here!"

The sound of car doors slamming and a panicked attempt to get the engine to splutter into life attracts the attention of the Agent and his mercenaries. The henchmen start to run towards the car, while the Agent lumbers more slowly in the same direction. "Someone's stealing the car. Stop them!" he barks.

"Er... the Agent is gaining on us," says Psy Kick, "which is odd given he's definitely morbidly obese, plus he and his henchmen are on foot while we're in a high performance car. Maybe we should start the engine and drive the car away."

"Not helping," shrieks Amadeo, "I'm trying to get this in gear..."

"What gear are you in?" enquires Skip.

"Rico is always in designer gear."

"I'll pull this gear stick out and hit you over..." Skip's threat to Rico is curtailed by the car suddenly shaking into life, as the engine purrs to the relief of all those inside the vehicle.

"Well done, Skip - that was it. Rico is pleased to have been of vital service to his teammates once again."

But although the engine has now started, the car is stuck, juddering to a halt on the same spot. Amadeo yells, "Quick.

The brake is still on. We need to find the button that releases the handbrake."

By now one of the Agent's henchmen has almost reached the car window. "Hey you, the one with the girl's hair!" he bellows. Rico places his hand to one side of his mouth and whispers, "Hey Skip, I think he's talking to you."

"And I'm talking to you, Rico, as you're the nearest to the green button," says Amadeo. "Please press it to release the handbrake now!"

"Hey, I'm his captain, I'll follow any instruction my manager gives me, not you. I am the one designated to carry out his orders."

"Rico has better vision than you. That is why Amadeo has selected Rico for this vital task, not you. Maybe Amadeo is thinking of crowning Rico as this team's captain. My fans would like that."

Rico and Skip rear up into a fight, like rutting stags on their hind legs - too busy to release the handbrake. A henchman reaches the car and the palm of his hand suddenly appears slammed flat against the back window, causing the foosballers to gasp in shock. "Well, that's *Titanic* ruined for me," remarks Loco.

"Oh for goodness sake, the Stripes are a bunch of idiots. How you can beat anyone is beyond me. Once again, it has to be a Claret to the rescue," snaps Gregor.

The henchman is now pounding on the back window. Trapped inside the stationary car, Amadeo and the foosballers are expecting him to break inside at any second. Gregor presses the button. But it does not release the handbrake. The car stays stubbornly still. But if the vehicle remains motionless, the henchman unexpectedly shoots away backwards because the button Gregor presses has activated the automatic boot release mechanism. The momentum of the boot shooting up flicks away the henchman who flies towards a soft squelchy landing in a pile of rotting turnips.

Psy Kick decides to take charge. "As my name implies, I am psychic. Press the orange button - that will release the brake." Amadeo presses it and the windscreen wipers come on. "OK, I meant to say purple one." The passenger window starts to open. "Definitely the blue one." The car horn sounds, immediately giving away their position. The other two henchmen, and even the waddling Agent, are now almost within touching distance of the car. "It's the white button!" continues Psy Kick. Amadeo presses the white button, and the brake is deactivated.

Instantaneously the car lurches forward like an animal suddenly released from a pen making a bolt for freedom. Seizing their chance to escape, Amadeo presses down the accelerator as deep as it will go and the car bumps along the dirt track heading for the rubbish tip's exit. "Told you it was the white button. I truly am psychic," boasts Psy Kick.

"It was the very last remaining option of all the buttons!" observes Skip.

"Actually, that was the button that Rico said you should press. Sometimes my genius is a burden."

"You certainly press my buttons," adds Skip. But his overwhelming feeling is of relief, not anger, as they speed away from the Agent - watching an angry fat man with a fat cigar becoming ever smaller in their rear-view mirror.

"Will we ever see our colleagues again?" asks Loco forlornly, "and the rest of the Pinks?"

"Clarets!" shouts Gregor predictably.

"And where's he taking my men?" asks Skip. "And Gregor's men the P... P..."

"Go on, say it," snarls Gregor.

"P... P... Players in the other side."

"At last. Thank you. That was a pleasant surprise," says Gregor contentedly.

"Yeah... the Pinks!"

Amadeo decides that dispensing some important information about each side's teammates might curtail the bickering and raises his voice to gain the foosballers' attention. "We know the exact place where they are going to be. If you paid attention then you heard the Agent say who he's collecting them for. So we're going to the same place where your teammates are heading. Let's go."

Landing lights spelling out a huge 'H' attract Flash's helicopter down to the light source like a giant moth. "This is where your mansion is - 35 seconds flying time? Why couldn't we have just walked?" asks Lara. "Why don't you international super villains ever care about the environment?"

"I refuse to do anything without a sponsor. Which can get awkward - my shower company stalled over an increased contract renewal and I couldn't shower for a fortnight." Lara's nose, already at quite a high angle, is turned up even more at Flash. "Now, let me give you a tour of my palace. The first room here is my master bedroom - I won't show you that at this stage as it's usually the final destination for my visitors after an evening with Flash. If you get my drift - as the snowplough driver once said to the lady on a pavement. Ha ha ha! I am magnificently witty."

"I think we may need to start the tour with the bathroom", ventures Lara.

"Er, OK, but why the bathroom?" asks Flash.

"So I can puke," Lara replies.

"Ha ha, you are quite a feisty one. Of course, please notice I have added mirrored ceilings to just about every room in my mansion... oh, you're going to be sick again?"

Flash claps his hands and automatically curtains close, lights dim and romantic piano keys tinkle through hidden speakers. "Lara, you are such a classy lady, so much classier than that boy who has never grown up, who plays with his toy footballers all day. Why don't you and I form a bond?"

He leads Lara into an opulent vestibule displaying numerous statues. It resembles a museum entrance rather than a home. Several of the statues are, somewhat immodestly, of Flash himself. "Wow, footballers have such good taste. This place is unbelievable - it makes Liberace's palace look understated," Lara sighs. "Thank you very much," Flash responds, failing to recognise even entry-level sarcasm.

"I see you've sensibly fitted twenty metre high doors - always useful to have a giraffe flap," she observes.

"Yes, thank you," Flash replies, oblivious to Lara's sarcasm.

"I can see the designers have followed their brief of 'flamboyant vulgarity'."

"I'm pleased you like it, Lara."

"Hmm… I see you've had a stair-lift installed on your marble staircase. Is that in case Wayne Rooney stays over one night and pulls?" asks Lara mischievously. "Oh you have some bookshelves," she continues. "Hmm…though you only have one book."

"That's my autobiography," proclaims Flash proudly, "though I haven't read it myself yet."

Lara picks the book up and opens it, before remarking, "I see you've dedicated your book to yourself." Flash nods, "Of course. Who else was worthy enough?"

9

Amadeo and the foosballers soon arrive at Flash's mansion in the Agent's requisitioned limo. Panting with exhaustion after sprinting across the vast gardens to the back of the house, Amadeo is only capable of pronouncing one word at a time. "Come... on... we'll... try... and ... get ... in... around... the... back." The scale of the house and gardens resembles a stately home or royal mansion. Amadeo has lifted the lid from the shoebox and the foosballers climb out onto Flash's expansive rear lawn.

Skip tries to help raise Amadeo's mood. "Yeah, you're a much better catch than Flash. Apart from having a bigger house, better car, higher paid job, celebrity status and millions of adorning fans 'cos of his natural talent and good looks, I don't know what Lara sees in him that you haven't got." Skip's speech is not warmly received by Amadeo. "OK, I'm not helping as much as I want to, am I?" Skip concedes.

"No," says Amadeo firmly, before addressing all the foosballers who have now arrived at the back entrance to the grandiose mansion. "Right, it's very important you remain safe and secure while I try and get inside. We don't want Flash stealing you too. So stay out of sight."

"I just feel that we owe Amadeo," Skip says to the others. "He's done so much for us. Our power is literally in his hands."

"He's got a good engine," says Rico, touching his heart.

"We're coming with you, Amadeo!" Skip shouts out as Amadeo is about to replace the lid on their box.

"Er, that's great guys. Really touched and everything. But

you do realise there's usually a minimum height requirement for guerrilla break-ins to liberate damsels in distress from super villains' lairs."

"Oh, is that a pop at my height?" asks Skip. "I never thought you're be heightist, man," adds a musing Loco. "The scorpion is deadlier than the elephant."

"Er… that depends on context, Loco. If a scorpion trod on me I'd fancy my chances of survival. But I wouldn't fancy your chances of survival if Flash trod on you."

"We're a team, man. There's no 'me' in team," says Rico.

"You mean there's no 'I' in team," says Skip, "In fact, there is a 'me' in team - well, there's an 'm' and 'e'."

"But there is an 'I' in Rico, which is fitting since I, Rico, am often the team."

"Right, I'm going to batter him. You'll discover there's an 'i' in fist - and a fist in your eye," threatens Skip.

"Stop it!" shouts Amadeo. "Clearly I can't trust you not to fight if left alone here in a box, so I'm going to allow you to accompany me on my mission inside. Don't make me regret that decision, OK?"

The foosballers erupt into a collective "Hurray!"

"But you can only come with me on one condition - you stick together as a team. OK, two conditions. And you promise you will all be very careful. Where we're going is bound to be dangerous. So stay here. And keep quiet and out of sight."

The foosballers cheer again.

"I said stay quiet!"

Amadeo suddenly looks pensive. "We have a problem, guys, a big problem. Or perhaps I should say we have a challenge."

"There are no challenges, only problems," says Loco.

"OK, we can agree on the semantics later. But first we need to figure out how to break into Flash's house. And quickly. I'm going to have a scan around the gardens to see if I can find anything lying around that may help with a spot of breaking and entering. Lara looked terrified when she was taken by Flash with his chopper. She's in grave danger, probably suffering horribly now, enduring a terrible, woeful time."

10

"More vintage champagne and quails' eggs, Lara?" asks a suave Flash at the very moment Amadeo and his pocket-sized companions are formulating a fearless plan to rescue her from the evil clutches of the superstar.

"Yeah, don't mind if I do," replies Lara. "And these lobster vol-au-vents are divine. Are there any more?"

"Yes, of course, I'll fetch you some. More caviar and a top-up in the meantime?"

Inside Flash's mansion Lara is enjoying the catering. But she is still determined to foil Flash and his evil plans. "You realise you have to let the villagers have their village back."

Flash does not like this sudden change in the conversation. "Oh, I think you'll find it is MY village, not theirs. Don't make me fetch the paperwork."

"Look, Flash," implores Lara, "you captain the world's greatest football side, the Grandmasters. You have money, fame, success, more than adequate property - look around you. You even have your own museum. Dedicated to, er, yourself. With specially commissioned statues of, um, you. I'm sure that's normal and healthy. So why do you want to own everything?"

Flash waits a few seconds before responding, hoping the pause will provide additional gravitas to his words: "There is nothing sitting in this palace that I would like to own as much as you."

"Flash, you don't own a person. And besides, you know I like Amadeo."

"I knew it!" Flash snaps, "he beat me once. Well I won't let it happen again. Not in MY village. He puts his hands around

Lara's neck. "Get off me!" Lara's lands a perfectly struck free kick between the sticks, kicking Flash in the…

"…arrghh… my unspeakables," he shrieks, two octaves higher than usual.

"You deserved that," says Lara unrepentantly.

"I think you'd better go, Lara. Why not have a walk around your village you claim to care about so much? While you still have the opportunity."

This is too much for Lara and she screams at him: "Flash you truly are a massive…"

Ding dong, ding dong.

It is the sound of the mansion's loud - and predictably larger than necessary - doorbell.

"And a complete," Lara continues, "and utter off the scale…"

Ding dong, ding dong.

"You total…"

Ding dong, ding dong.

The mansion doorbell continues to be rung impatiently.

"I hate it when the doorbell goes," says an irritated Flash, "it's about a twelve minute walk from here to the front door. Oh well, better set off."

Twelve minutes later, the Agent is let in.

"What took you so long? I heard your limo pulling into the driveway ages ago."

The Agent wobbles inside, the door opened just enough for his generously-girthed, built-for-comfort frame to slip through. If he was expecting "hello" as a greeting, then he should be used to being disappointed by Flash by now. Instead he starts to explain why it had taken him so long to arrive. "We encountered a few car difficulties at the dump. We had to phone for a taxi."

"I don't care about your difficulties, minion. Well?" demands Flash, dispensing with any greetings, small-talk, offers of a drink or general civility.

"We had our car stolen, but it appears to be parked outside your house, Flash."

"Then that's convenient for you leaving, isn't it, which I hope you will do soon. Immediately after you've given me what I asked for."

The Agent is slow to respond.

"Well?" Flash reiterates, "what about the foosball players? Where are they? Speak, imbecile!"

The Agent prepares himself to deliver a statement Flash will not like. "I've captured the foosball table from the café demolition like you ordered, and most of the players are in this bag."

Snatching the bag, Flash throws it across the room like a Christmas present that has failed to meet a spoilt child's standards. Fortunately for the foosballers inside, they experience a soft landing on the upholstery of a priceless antique chaise-longue.

"Most of them? I heard the word 'most'! You useless cretin - why are some players missing? Where are the other players, moron? Why do I pay you? I should get another agent. What's your agency called? Cretins-R-Us?"

"I think we may have our wires crossed, Flash. I managed to get…" This is as far as the Agent's sentence is allowed to get until Flash shouts him down. "My wires are as straight and untangled as it's possible for wires to be. If there are any wires crossed, it's at your end and you did the crossing. I suggest you bring me the rest of the foosball players NOW! Oh, and also bring me the wires once you've uncrossed them - so I can strangle your useless fat neck with them. Now, depart minion. AND FIND THOSE FOOSBALL PLAYERS!!"

The Agent limps away without responding to Flash. He is smart enough to know that attempting to reason with the unreasonable is futile.

Back in the Living Room - or rather Living Room Number 9 - Lara tries to establish Flash's motives. "What do you want with harmless toys?" she asks.

"They were the reason I lost the only game I have ever been beaten in. And so I have a plan - OK, mainly a vengeful plan, I grant you - but a plan nevertheless to crush the foosball players and use their materials, distil their essence of victory into my studs. With stronger studs I can trample on my opponents more easily. If I achieve the perfect football boots for the perfect footballer - me! - my power will be limitless. Currently I am only adored; but I want to be worshipped."

"You're mad," says a startled Lara. "How is crushing a toy footballer going to give you perfect studs?"

"Talking of perfect studs, Lara, do you like me, or do you really like me?"

"Don't make me kick you again…" she says, raising her right-foot with considerable back lift.

11

Tiny faces belonging to the foosball players appear outside a window of Flash's living room, peering in at the scene taking place inside.

"There's Lara. And Flash. We must help her!" Skip steps up onto a pebble to address his men. "Members of my team, and the Pinks…"

"…Clarets!" snaps Gregor with fraying patience.

"Right, I'm your captain - so let's talk tactics. Specifically tactical ideas for gaining entrance to Flash's mansion. Firstly we need a name for the operation. It's an operation to rescue Lara. Any ideas? Anyone?"

"How about Operation Rescue Lara?" pitches Gregor.

"That's OK, but a bit pinky for my tastes."

"How about 'Operation Piper at the Gates of Dawn?'" offers Loco.

"Er… yeah. Maybe we'll go with Operation Rescue Lara. Now pay very careful attention. Tactics and strategy are everything. We must stick to a carefully crafted game plan, use our heads and retain our shape and discipline at all times. I want my midfielders to… oh no, you're all going ahead, rushing in and doing your own thing, aren't you?!"

Skip is correct. The players have linked hands and are running as hard as they can towards the reinforced glass window of Flash's living room. They rebound painfully off the glass with a dull thud, dropping to the ground. "That's a headache a couple of junior aspirin won't cure," sighs Skip. The impact is not heard inside by Flash or Lara, such is the impenetrable thickness of the strengthened glass.

"Wow, that's some strong glass sheet, dude," announces the dreadlocked Loco. "Anyone got any snacks?"

"You morons," Gregor curses them.

"Who are you calling a moron, moron?" Skip snaps back.

"You are both morons. Rico knows this."

"Really? I'm a moron. Well you're the biggest moron. If all the morons in the world wanted a ruler, you'd be unanimously elected as their leader - the morons' moron."

"Rico is not listening to this. He doesn't speak moron so cannot converse with you."

"That's it, says Skip, "I'm making a fist."

Sensing they are unlikely to rescue Lara with this attitude, Loco steps in. "Stop arguing, boys. We're all on the same side. We must bond. Stick together like stick insects stuck in a sticky situation on a sticky stick. And that means YOU Skip have to work with HIM Rico. And both of you have to work with him the pink one. So everyone form a circle of respect and share one good quality you admire about each other."

"I'm gonna thump him…" rages Skip.

"You know, he's right," says Gregor.

"It's either strength in unity or weakness in our disarray," Loco announces.

Skip nods sagely. "OK, Loco's right. So come on team, let's figure out how to break into this mansion and commence Operation Lara Rescue."

"Operation Rescue Lara" says Gregor, correcting him.

"Well, I prefer Operation Lara Rescue, you pink git."

"It's Claret not pink!"

"Sorry. You Claret git!"

Gregor and Skip press their foreheads together, on the verge of trading blows.

"Guys, let's harmonise as a team. You've just agreed to work together, dudes." The other foosballers nod that Loco is right.

Cometh the hour, cometh the Korean midfield maestro. Psy Kick strolls purposefully forward towards the door and looks up at the numerical keypad above him. "Psy Kick can summon the ageless powers of oriental wisdom and work out the entry combination."

"Of courses," yells Skip with enthusiasm, "Psy Kick is my psychic side-kick."

"That's easy for you to say," offers Gregor. Psy Kick raises his hand indicating he requires silence to concentrate. A reverential quiet descends, the foosballers line up with arms linked over each other's shoulders - like a team in the centre-circle enduring a penalty shootout. The tension matches that of a penalty shootout that has just entered sudden death kicks.

Psy Kick tunes his mind like a radio into the frequency of psychic energy, channelling his dynamic thought power, his brain whirling with supercomputing powers, a cryptologist cracking the seemingly impenetrable code. "I've got it," he announces triumphantly. "It's a keypad with some numbers on."

"I thought you said you used to work at Bletchley Park?" Skip says.

"I did," replies Psy Kick, "they had a foosball table in the staff canteen."

Amadeo has returned from seeking any stick or implement he can find in the garden that may help them break in, in time to see the foosballers spontaneously charge towards the window again. "Oh no, I told you to be careful and stay out of sight," he sighs, prepared to reel at the sound of tiny heads hitting a glass wall. But the sound - and his anticipated flinch - never occurs because at the moment when unavoidable impact is imminent, Flash opens the French doors, allowing the foosballers to continue their run inside unimpeded.

"Let's enjoy the moonlight in my gardens," purrs Flash to Lara as he steps outside, oblivious to the tiny foosballers rushing almost under his feet from the lawn onto his thick shag pile carpet. Amadeo ducks behind a thick rose bush. "Tailored terrains and personally landscaped by a top garden designer. Nice bush, eh?"

"Pardon?" asks Lara.

"My personal gardener has created several images of me in topiary. Would you like to see them?"

"Flash, I don't think it's normal to have recreated yourself as a giant bush."

Flash raises his hand and moves it to the left, as if batting away Lara's last comment. "Not for a mere mortal, perhaps, but I am Flash."

"Yes you are. Too flash for most people's liking."

Again, Flash doesn't react to Lara's obvious put-down. It does not occur to him that anyone might object to his self-aggrandisement.

Then Lara lets out a scream – exactly when she really didn't mean to. "Arrrgghhh!!"

"What is it, Lara? What have you seen?" asks Flash anxiously.

"Er… er… Oh, I just saw one of the images of your greatness created in topiary."

"Yes, it is rather magnificent, isn't it? Flash agrees, "although the subject matter automatically enables the sculpture to depict perfection."

Lara has screamed because she is shocked to have spotted Amadeo in the garden. But she recovers quickly. "Actually, do let me see your magnificent self-depicting topiary," she says as non-sarcastically as she can manage - which still sounds quite sarcastic. Hoping to distract the megalomaniac and allow Amadeo to remain unseen, she prolongs her ruse: "Just remembered… um… that… I love horticultural sculpture. Yes, that's it," she concludes a tad unconvincingly.

"Why of course. I think you're forgetting all about that sad loser boyfriend of yours. I bet you haven't thought about or seen him for a while, have you?"

"No, I haven't seen him for ages."

"Forget about him Lara. He's such an irritatingly little prick."

Amadeo seizes the moment while Lara is distracting Flash.

Jumping out of the rose bush, he pricks himself on several rose thorns but bolts towards Flash's living room through the open French windows. There he finds the foosballers, hiding in the carpet. "My hands are full of irritating little pricks," he complains

"That's because you must have picked up the Pink team," Skip suggests.

"It's Clarets. How many times?!" snarls Gregor.

"Really guys, I need you to stop bickering and help. Please pull these rose thorns out of my hands," begs Amadeo. The foosballers select a thorn each and clasp their little hands around it. Then they heave. "Hea-ve, hea-ve, hea-ve!" calls Skip as they pull backwards away from Amadeo's hands, straining like a tug of war team. One by one, the thorns are removed.

"Thanks, guys. I knew it was right to bring you along."

"We have to keep your magic hands fit for our next game, boss!" says Skip.

"There's the others! Look!" Rico has spotted the other missing foosball players - their captured teammates they last saw when the Agent abducted them at the rubbish dump - unceremoniously dumped in a bag on Flash's chaise-longue.

Meanwhile in the garden Lara is continuing to perform her cunning duplicity. When Flash announces, "It's getting a bit chilly out here, so let's go back inside," she realises she must at all costs keep distracting him to stop him discovering Amadeo. "Er, Flash," she calls, changing tonal gears in her voice from sneery, through civil, to flatteringly interested, "please do show me the grand tour of your amazing home and how it helps a great player like you push the boundaries of greatness."

"Of course. I'm amazed you didn't ask me earlier."

Lara manages to restrain herself, though an audible squeak of revulsion does leak out.

"Let me show you my own personal laboratory, harnessing science to improve my greatness. Do you like science?" Flash asks perplexingly.

"Yes, I like science. Doesn't everyone? It would be hard not to like it."

"Oh good, I just thought I'd check, you being a… er..."

"Were you going to say girl?!" enquires Lara in a tone that suggests he had really, really better not have been.

"No, of course not. I'd never say that."

"Good," agrees Lara.

"I was going to say… with you being a woman. 'Girl' would have been sexist and patronising," reasons Flash.

Lara decides that she will speak very loudly in order to warn Amadeo of their imminent arrival back indoors. "This really is amazing décor. I bet the taste police have issued several arrest warrants," she remarks to Flash, who replies with an impervious, "thanks, pleased you like it - though I'm afraid you will never be able to afford it."

Her ruse works. Amadeo and the little guys hide as soon as they hear Flash and Lara approaching - this proves considerably easier for the foosballers than it does for Amadeo. While he lies flat behind the chaise-longue next to the skirting board, like a draft excluder in front of a door, the foosballers merely scurry underneath the furniture.

"Oh, I'll be needing these to show you an experiment I am about to conduct. It will really impress you," boasts Flash as he collects the bag of containing the abducted foosballers.

Flash beckons to Lara to follow him as they descend a steep staircase. "You are truly honoured to be seeing my underground laboratory," he informs her. After keying in entry codes on three separate air locked security doors equipped with the latest facial scanning and iris recognition, he announces, "this is my top secret science centre - one of the most airtight and secure areas in… oh, how has next door's cat got in here again? Shoo, off you go moggy."

"Wow, this is like an underground lair," says Lara, genuinely taken aback by the scale of the facility.

Flash's cavernous laboratory is equipped with several science stations. A separate experiment appears to be running at each one. Lara immediately suspects that these experiments are not being conducted for the power of good - quite the opposite, she supposes. She is also astounded that Flash would possess sufficient scientific knowledge to conduct such experiments - she is surrounded by frothing beakers, oscillating needles, flickering spectroscopes, hissing valves and flashing screens. This is vertiginously high hi-tech.

But these individual experiment stations are mere sideshow attractions to a huge machine in the centre of Flash's basement. Here a conventional-looking conveyor belt rises steeply towards the ceiling at an acute angle, where it overhangs a cauldron containing a corkscrew-shaped blade emerging vertically from a vat of bubbling chemicals. A series of cog wheels drive the conveyor belt and its unfortunate cargo upwards towards an inevitable drop into the deadly mechanism at the machine's core.

"What's that machine for?" asks Lara apprehensively.

"That is an extractor," replies Flash.

"What does it extract?"

"The essence of victory. I'll demonstrate it in action shortly. But first a tour of my other scientific innovations. Why not let my chief scientist be your personal tour guide? This is Nerdina. She was instrumental in developing all the powerful experimental technology you see here. Well, she helped a bit in shaping MY visions."

"Oh... hello." Lara is surprised to greet someone else in Flash's villainous underworld cavern.

"I'm called Nerdina. Yes, I know what you're thinking - surely all mad scientists fixated on destroying the world are male. Well, sister, not anymore."

Nerdina is wearing a white coat and safety goggles. Her lab coat's top pocket is filled with a rainbow selection of coloured pens. She is in her early 20s and wears her dark brown hair steeply up, secured tightly with multiple hairclips.

"You see, I can pointlessly wear a white lab coat too - like all scientists. Why a white coat? It's the worst possible practical colour in an experiment, always getting stained. Anyway, although I have glasses and my hair tied-up, on no account will I conform to the cliché of unwrapping it, swaying my head like I'm in a cheap shampoo commercial and allow everyone to notice the hidden potency of my beauty."

"Er... that's great," agrees Lara, not sure how to react.

"Nerdina here is brilliant, isn't she? She's by far my best henchman."

"Henchperson!" says Nerdina, sharply.

"It's so useful to have someone else do all the sciency stuff required to advance my vision. And she's totally evil too. Really, she is. I'm so lucky to have found her."

"Yes, I am totally evil. I'm sure my life would be much easier if I was nice, but I'm determined never to find out. Right, I need a pick-me-up - anyone got a puppy or kitten I can hurt for a bit?"

"Ha ha, isn't she great?" giggles Flash nervously, his jocular tone fading as he murmurs to himself, "that explains how that cat got in."

"Why did you decide to be an evil scientist for a living?" asks Lara.

"Well, I used to work for an investment bank, but then I just decided I needed to do something much more moral with my life," replies Nerdina.

"But why became a super villain aspiring to global-domination?" Lara presses.

"Well, I admit I didn't get the A-level grades I hoped for. I originally aspired to work in the ultimate laboratory for scientists."

"What, at CERN?"

"No, Laboratoire Garnier."

"Oh," says a genuinely surprised Lara.

"Some credit for ME at this point, please, says Flash. "Before she met me Nerdina was only intent on planning villainous domination on Rutland and a small part of South East Leicestershire. With my influence, I untethered her parochial ambitions and she is now planning global domination. Ha-ha-mwahahaha-ha… oh that laugh really DOES hurt your throat."

"I am sick of the ludicrous and perfidious sexism in super villainy," declares Nerdina. "A world-owning megalomaniacal villain can be female too, you know. Just don't call me 'feisty'. Don't ever call me 'feisty'! Women are capable of evil plotting and scheming for total global destruction and annihilation just as much as any male super baddie, and I will destroy the world…. oh drat, I've just chipped another nail."

"I think you've fundamentally misunderstood feminism," suggests Lara.

"Shut it, Snow White," snaps Nerdina, before her voice rises into an impassioned crescendo; "I will take over the entire world. You'll see. Then my school science teacher will be sorry once I have enslaved the world. Ha ha, bwa-ha-ha, mwaha-ha-ha, haw-ha-ha, bwah-ha-ha, mwaha-ha-ha-ha…"

"Oh, her evil laugh is so good, isn't it?" gushes Flash.

But suddenly Nerdina has a pronounced change of tone, "Oh wow, is THAT the time already? I need to be at the dry cleaners before they close and I promised myself I wouldn't be late for Zumba class again. Bye everyone. Nice to meet you, Lara. See you in the morning, Flash."

As Nerdina hurries up the stairs Flash remarks, "best work

experience henchman… henchperson… I've ever had. Really does restore your faith in today's young people."

"She seems feisty," says Lara.

"I heard that!" Nerdina shouts disapprovingly from the stairwell.

"Allow me to continue the tour and show you MY creations and MY designs…" Flash is interrupted by a loud feminine cough from the stairwell, "built with some limited input from Nerdina, obviously," he continues, beckoning Lara to follow him. "Everything here is designed with the latest innovations in nanotechnology to make me become even more perfect. The cutting edge just got a lot sharper."

Lara decides against pointing out that as a philosophical entity, perfection is hardly susceptible to improvement. She also considers engaging Flash in a philosophical discussion would be roughly akin to teaching a housefly irregular French verbs.

Besides, Flash only has one topic of conversation that he engages in: himself. "Here these white eagles are flying around in a cage trailing long lengths of soft down fabric for my new lightweight air-porous football kit," he boasts.

"Wow," exclaims Lara, "and this?"

"This is where doves are testing the lightest type of material for my shorts and socks. They live and die here. If a small pretty bird can help me to achieve greatness, its life has been worthwhile. I'm just ramming home an obvious metaphor here," he adds. With this he strokes Lara's hair, a move that her body language reveals is not exactly welcome.

An eagle flies towards them, screeching. Flash bats at the bird to shoo it away. "Why must Flash always have to fend off the birds, eh?"

"Here," Flash continues, oblivious to Lara's interest being real or faked, "testing my boots, we have ostriches capable of killing a man with one kick. See, they are hybrids who have football boots for beaks."

An ostrich, its head hooden by a boot, repeatedly bangs it

against the glass of the cage in a futile attempt to dislodge it.

"I like telling them to 'shoo'. Why doesn't anyone find that funny?" asks Flash.

Lara attempts a fake laugh at Flash's feeble witticism. She has to try much harder than she realised.

"Yes, I created all of this science myself," says an increasingly boastful Flash as he puts the bag of foosballers on the floor.

"All by yourself?" checks Lara

"Yes… well, with some minimal help from Nerdina, but I should take the credit really," he says immodestly.

While Flash is looking at the ostriches, Lara subtly dips her knees, stoops down, and picks up the bag of foosballers. "This is an amazing place, Flash. And please do show me what is over here." Assuming that Flash is happy talking about himself indefinitely, she slips the foosballers into her shoulder bag hopefully unnoticed.

"Yes, the arts can appreciate me with paintings, songs and sculptures - so it's only fair that I allow science an opportunity to acclaim me too. That is what this laboratory does."

"Er… yes, I so see that, Flash."

"The bag please, Lara."

"What bag, Flash?" asks Lara, knowing that the artificial innocence in her voice is not going to work.

"You know perfectly well, Lara, I am referring to the bag of foosball players you just slipped into your shoulder bag."

"Oh, that bag." Lara pulls it out of her bag, aware that she also now quickly needs to pull an escape out of the bag too if she is to return the foosballers safely to Amadeo.

Flash snatches the bag of kidnapped players from Lara.

"What are you doing?!" she shouts.

Flash takes the bag and its contents over to the machine in the middle of his basement lair. "Time for you to see The Extractor machine extract, Lara."

"What's it going to do?" she asks, feeling profoundly uncomfortable.

"Well, I… with Nerdina assisting a teeny bit… have calculated the exact length and angle of this conveyor belt to drop its cargo at the optimum speed and position into the chemical solution below. The blade reduces anything I put into the vat to a sticky pulp, allowing its essence to be captured via a fusing process with the chemical reaction. Nerdina - who helped a miniscule amount, in fact her contribution was nothing really compared to mine - knows the details. It involves lots of sciency things and, you know, sciency stuff."

"Right, of course. Sciency stuff. Very technically explained," says Lara sarcastically. Flash, not for the first time, remains immune to her facetiousness.

"The final stage of the machine is Victorian technology - steam to distil the purified essence. That, in essence, is how I obtain the essence. Wow, I still surprise myself daily just how clever I am. Now I need to turn the machine on, and MY creation - built and designed by ME… oh, where did Nerdina leave the instructions? Oh yes, I asked her to put a post-it note on the start button. Here it is." Flash pushes the button marked by a note declaring "It's this one to start it!" (positioned next to a red button with a post-it proclaiming "this button stops it") and the machine awakes from its dormancy.

"As I was saying, here is where I distil the essence of the footballers who were responsible for my only ever draw."

"Draw? You drew 4-3?"

"Yes, a, er, 4-3, draw."

"You're mad… er… maddeningly attractive, Flash," says Lara manipulatively. And turns away from Flash to grimace a sick face.

"I know. This experimental extraction will ensure my boots have the strongest possible metal studs imbued with the essence of victory. By melting down those minuscule leaden foosballers I will achieve the strongest studs ever created. With these studs I can trample on my opponents better and crush them and their dreams. Talking of studs, Lara, how do you feel to be in my presence?"

"Repelled," answers Lara immediately, under her breath. "Oh honoured, Flash, of course."

"Time for the little toy footballers to drop in on The Extractor's pulping mechanism!" Flash declares in horribly sadistic tones. One of the foosballers clings to the corner of the upturned bag but Flash easily shakes him loose and he too drops onto the moving metallic belt to join his teammates.

"No, you can't just crush them!" protests Lara.

"Hmm... Let's examine the evidence. My tiny toy footballers are moving on my conveyor belt towards my crusher to be turned into my studs for my football boots. Yip, looks like I can."

"You're evil."

"Now, now, Lara. We both know this whole hard-to-get role playing thing you're doing is an act. See how the conveyor belt continues to carry the players towards destination crusher."

"No! Please! I just remembered that I really like you, Flash. Women, eh? What are we like? So if you could just stop your lovely death machine," she implores.

"I can see through your subterfuge - you're being knowingly ironic. Everyone can see that. Do you know a newspaper critic once had the ignorant audacity to award me one star for a match performance. He'll be seeing more than one star if I ever meet him in a CCTV blindspot."

"Flash, it doesn't matter if not all the people idolise you as a genius. You have vast wealth and huge numbers of fans. So please stop the machine. Let me and the foosballers go."

Lara grabs at the button adorned with a post-it marked "Emergency Stop" - obviously written by Nerdina for Flash to follow only the simplest of instructions. Lara pushes the lever and the machine responds instantly by starting to slow down. "Lara, take your hand away from that button now!" orders Flash.

"What?" says Lara innocently, "do you mean this button?"

"That's right, Lara. The one which stops the conveyor belt.

And we don't want to stop the slow and very painful crushing of the foosballers who beat me, do we. After all, I must have my new studs."

"Right," says Lara, "so just to clarify, you mean don't push this button to turn the machine off now, like this. That's not what I'm supposed to do. OK, I know now."

While Flash emits a cry of exasperation, several tiny foosball players, bedecked in claret as well as green and yellow striped shirts, jump off the conveyor belt. But not everyone can escape. Mac the Keeper, the cap-wearing goalie, and Beville are stuck at the very top of the mechanism. Stranded at the conveyor belt's pinnacle they are far too high to jump to safety.

"What are you doing up there?" shouts Beville Beville to his stranded twin teammate.

"Realising I'm scared of heights!" replies Beville.

"Typical, caught out of position again," jeers his brother from lower down the belt.

"Right, time to distil some essence - my eau de cologne of victory!" announces Flash, before attempting a sinister evil laugh. "Haw-ha-ha-ha-hahaw… oh, that really hurts the throat." He pushes the start button and the machine suddenly purrs back into life. As the remaining foosballers are falling from the conveyor belt, some are already too far into the crushing machine to escape, bobbling hopelessly like barrels on the edge of Niagara Falls. "Looks like the Stripes are heading for a crushing defeat," smirks Flash. Lara knows she has to push the button back down to stop the machine.

"Hmmm… so once more, this is the button I should not push - like this. Oh, sorry, I've turned the machine off again. I'm just a girl so I don't know anything about machines; it's all too complicated for my little female brain… oh, I've just remembered that kittens exist… aren't kittens lovely?"

"OK, I get it, Lara. Girls can be smart too, and you don't want to crush and pulp the footballers," says Flash resignedly.

"Really? I thought I was being too subtle for you."

"Call me old fashioned, but I do believe women have their place. In your case that place is the broom cupboard. Come on!"

Flash grabs Lara by her trailing ponytail and pulls her like a dog reluctant to go for a walk until they reach a tiny broom cupboard.

"Get off me, you psycho!"

"You give me no choice, Lara. If you insist on sabotaging my creation, then not only are you risking my continued greatness, but you are also depriving my millions of fans from seeing me attain even greater perfection."

A key turns, locking the door and forcing her to watch Flash through a wire mesh panel in the broom cupboard door. "You'll be unsurprised to know that I'm not much of a fan of feminism. So you may want to use this time constructively to reacquaint yourself with brooms, hoovers, carpet cleaners, polishers and dusters. How can we describe all those things collectively? Oh yeah: women's work. Now, back to important business without interruption." Lara may at some future stage in her life be as angry again as she is right now, but she doubts that very much.

Flash stands in front of the machine's button, shielding it from Lara's view behind the door - and turns it on again. Lara screams at Flash, and pounds the door with her fists, knowing both gestures are ultimately pointless. Lara now realises that the foosballers cannot escape their crushing fate. If it is still not quite all over for them yet, then they are 5-0 down and the referee is looking at his watch.

12

Skip, Rico, Loco and Gregor have hitched a lift on Amadeo's shoulder as he runs from glitzy room to glitzy room in Flash's mansion. And there is an awful lot of over-the-top décor to see in this tawdry temple of tat. But now, hearing Lara's scream, they head in the direction of her voice: underground. Their timing is on the fortuitous side of lucky.

They rush down the steps, passing through the three doors Flash has carelessly left open and step over a startled cat who gives a hungry growl at Rico. "Rico does not think that lion is very friendly. Hey, Rico sees his old teammates. And some of his old foes - the Pinks!"

"It's the Clarets," interjects Gregor.

"Oh, and Rico can see Lara too. She is behind a door - probably hiding because she is embarrassed that her hair is not as magnificent as Rico's."

"Quickly, all your colleagues are on a conveyor belt, about to be fed into some sort of machine. We must save them," pleads Amadeo.

"Alas, it's too late, boss. We cannot reach them in time," Loco points out. "We are all stardust and each blinking star will one day be extinguished."

"I'll blinking extinguish you..." Skip starts to say, but applies the vocal brakes when he sees Amadeo's expression of sheer horror and dejection.

Amadeo sighs despairingly: "Loco is right. We can't get down there to Flash's machine in time." Then his voice springs back up in tone: "But we can save Lara. Come on, guys."

Struggling on the conveyor belt, the seemingly doomed foosballers tremble and judder along towards their inevitable fatal drop. The vibrations take Beville towards the edge of the conveyor belt where he despairingly grabs and holds onto the protruding end of a screw. Mustering all his strength, he succeeds in pulling out the screw. "Oh drat. I was hoping that would stop the machine," he wheezes.

"And how exactly did you think pulling out one tiny screw was going to stop a machine this powerful, you stupid ugly moron?" says an unimpressed Beville Beville, kicking away the screw to emphasise his displeasure.

"Hey, shut it, twin brother. Or I'll shut your pig ugly face myself," screams Beville at his sibling.

Mac the Keeper joins the conversation: "How can you call him ugly, Beville? He's your identical twin. He ain't ugly, he's your brother. Hey, that sounds good - someone should definitely do a song called that."

"He's so heavy!" exclaims Beville, breaking his brother's fall by catching him.

"No, I still think 'He ain't ugly' makes a better song title," chips in Mac the Keeper.

"Now, since our irreversible destiny is to fall into this crushing machine, may I once again strongly suggest screaming?" They both roar: "AARRRRRGGGHHH!"

Unknown to the Beville brothers, the screw Beville has removed and his brother has kicked away soars upwards. It rebounds off a protruding edge in the machine's internal workings and lands in a critical meeting point of two cog wheels. The result is that the wheels suddenly begin to grind, then stop, before vibrating with an alarmingly loud noise. Finally the cog wheels burst loose with a sudden jettisoning of released pressure, and fly straight into the control panel.

"I always knew Flash had a screw loose," quips Beville.

The conveyor belt now jolts to a complete halt. The loose screw, seemingly small and insignificant, has found its way into the workings of the giant machine and brought it to a shuddering stop. Then an ominous rattling sound, rising in volume, is heard from inside the contraption's central mechanism.

Loco has spotted what is happening. "Hey, everyone. See how a tiny screw of apparently no significance has brought down the giant destructive machine. It's a metaphor for the importance of the smallest cogs, how tiny foosballers can overcoming Flash. And how a lone act of small defiance can bring down The Man, man."

With the central drive belt bearing the main thrust of the machine now stuck, the shaking intensifies and the apparatus starts to shake dangerously. Flash's whole house is suddenly wobbling like a jelly in an earthquake. Ornaments, of the predictably tacky variety, start to vibrate and then fall from shelves and mantelpieces, smashing to the floor. Then one of Flash's statues, immodesty commissioned by himself of himself, topples over and breaks. "Nooooooooo…" Flash screams. One of his trophy cabinets capsizes in the vibrations, spilling its shattered contents. "No!!! Not my Johnstone Paint Trophy runners-up medals!" he squeals.

The reprieved foosballers jump free of the stalled conveyor belt just as Amadeo arrives to pick them up. "Guys, get into this box."

"Let's go, Amadeo," urges Skip, "before this places falls down and Flash spots us."

"Aren't you forgetting something?" Amadeo asks.

"Er… no… oh, if you want to rescue Lara too, then she's in that broom cupboard over there," says Skip. Amadeo turns the key and releases her. If not a kiss, then he was at least hoping for a 'thank you'; possibly even upgraded to a hug - but none of these are forthcoming. Instead Lara has a more immediate agenda in mind.

"Evacuate now!" she screams, mainly as a distraction to allow Amadeo and his foosballers to escape unnoticed in the pandemonium. "The entire house is going to blow up!" she cries. Lara's mock hysteria induces a sweaty panic in Flash.

"Save me, save me, save me - saving yourself is optional," he shouts in horror-filled consternation.

"Yeah," says Lara coolly, "the whole house will explode shortly, or we could just push this button here, the one I earlier demonstrated that stops and starts the machine and that Nerdina has marked with a big post-in stating 'Emergency Stop'." Lara calmly pushes the button down with her index finger and the machine obligingly judders to a halt.

"Oh yeah. That button. Yeah, good job," say Flash.

13

The next day Flash calls a press conference on the village green. "How lucky the happy residents of this village are, to have the world's most advanced football stadium built here," he declares. "It will be constructed at record speed. Your village has been a justifiable sacrifice in the construction of a new era."

"Just a minute, Flash." It is Amadeo. "How can the villagers be lucky, happy residents when there aren't going to be any villagers left? Because you can't have any villagers without a village."

"Oh it's you again."

"Yes, that's right, Flash, it's me again. The person who once beat you."

Flash does not welcome this sentiment being expressed in public. "What? I think you need to work in a more ventilated area. Clearly your brain's been affected by some fumes as I have never lost a game in my life."

Flash puffs out his chest, and selects full arrogance mode. It is his default setting. "I have never lost a game. And people WILL want this giant stadium so that they can see the greatest ever footballer appearing in this village. That's right - the greatest footballing genius in the game's history will play here in MY village."

"Wow, the former Grimsby Town, Scunthorpe and Boston United midfielder Mike Brolly is going to play for our village team?" Spencer asks Moxey excitedly. "Home win," replies Moxey.

"ME! It's me! ME!! I'm the greatest ever footballer! ME!!"

screams Flash, providing himself with an opportunity once again to use one of his favourite words: "ME!" "And may I take this opportunity to reiterate that I have never been beaten?" adds Flash with a further generous helping of hubris.

"Wait a minute! Flash, I beat you once," says Amadeo with surging confidence, a sense of injustice added to his courage by the lie he has just heard.

"I think you'll find… whatever your name is, I honestly can't remember but I'm sure it's something tiresome… THAT I HAVE NEVER BEEN BEATEN."

"Yes, you were. I beat you here in this village. And I hereby challenge you to a re-match. And my name is Amadeo."

Everyone present emits a collective gasp like a punctured barrage balloon. Father Dick Dawkins removes his hat and places it in front of his chest as a sign of respect for the inevitable death ahead. Several other villagers cross themselves. Meanwhile the village church bell again tolls solemnly. Dogs howl mournfully. The sun disappears behind a dark menacing cloud. Lara's eyes roll skywards. She is silently cursing Amadeo.

"So, the wimpy little toy football champ wants a re-match, does he?" sneers Flash, revelling in this development.

"Yes I do. And I'll beat you, Flash. Again. Just like I did last time."

"OK then, bring it on… I've actually forgotten your name again. It's the village team at home to my team: the all-conquering invincible global superstars the Grandmasters. Can you predict the outcome?"

"Home win," opines Moxey.

"I accept your challenge," declares Flash.

"Very well. That's good, isn't it?" says Amadeo.

"But not at a kid's game. I challenge you to a real football match."

"A real football game?" gulps Amadeo.

"You always were a coward. And guess what? You always will be," says Flash dismissively.

"Oh yeah?" This has angered Amadeo. A lot. "Name the day!"

"Wait!" yells Lara as she runs through the crowd. Amadeo is suddenly relieved as he knows Lara is clever enough to get him out of the mess he has just created. There is no way he can raise a local team to beat Flash at proper full scale football. Lara to the rescue, he thinks, she'll know what to do and how to skilfully cancel the ludicrous challenge he has just somehow signed up to. Amadeo sits down on a bench, confident that Lara will know how to settle the situation, mop up the mess his impulsiveness has caused.

As a roving microphone is handed to her, Lara finally speaks: "To make the challenge more interesting," she says to Flash, "shall we go double or quits?"

"What?!" Amadeo shrieks in shock, involuntarily standing up like he had just received a potent electrical charge from his seat.

"Why don't we say that if Amadeo and his village team win, then you give us back our village?" Lara suggests.

Amadeo now feels such a combination of abject shock, surprise and fear that he realises that even though his mouth is open, and he is actually screaming "Nooo! Are you mad Lara?" his brain has forgotten to get him to say it out loud. That's how disorientated he has become. Which is very disorientated indeed.

"What's the matter, Flash? Lost your nerve?" Lara continues to grind Flash down until he responds the way she wants. "Perhaps you're the biggest coward after all?" she says provocatively, before adding quietly under her breath, "surely you haven't become impervious to transparent psychological tricks?"

"I accept your challenge! It shall be the match staged as the grand opening of the new Astro Dome stadium. Oh, that's not right - did I say 'match'? - I meant, of course, 'mis-match'. Ha ha ha! You will be humiliated. Crushed. Destroyed. Annihilated.

Smashed. Demolished, Extirpated… er… has anyone got a Thesaurus please?"

"Right, that's that then. We've better go house hunting for a new village," says the Guv'nor to the nodding agreement of surrounding locals.

"No need as we're going to get the village back, after Amadeo beats Flash!" proclaims Chester. This, it has to be said, is a somewhat minority view.

14

Outside the press conference, Flash signs autographs before stepping into a waiting black limo. Lara approaches Amadeo to ask him a question: "Why did you come to Flash's mansion last night?"

"To rescue you," Amadeo replies, hoping for some serious gratitude.

"To rescue me? Like I'm a damsel in distress?"

"Er, kind of, I suppose, no… I mean…"

"Should I have let my hair down from a high window so you could climb up and rescue me from a tower?"

"OK, I'm getting a strong reading on the sarcasm meter."

Lara sighs, before informing him very clearly: "I didn't need rescuing, Amadeo. And you've put yourself in danger messing with Flash. He is much more powerful, stronger and better connected than you, and very probably a psychopath. Now he is even more determined to destroy our village. Especially after we destroyed his mad laboratory."

"But I thought…"

"What did you think? That because you were brave" - Lara adopts an infantile voice - "ah be-cause you were a bravey-wavey likkle boy you would rescue me."

"Er… I guess. I don't know."

"And then I would automatically fall in love with you as a consequence?"

"Yes… Oh, that's the wrong thing to say, isn't it?"

"The world is not a fairy story, Amadeo. If you spent more time in the real world rather than retreating from it with your toy football obsession, you would know that. And be better equipped to deal with it."

This hurts Amadeo. "Oh yeah? Well, how well do you understand the real world if you just bet the village - the continued existence of our homes and businesses - on a real football match we will likely lose 100-nil?"

"We were going to lose the village anyway, Amadeo. We have to make the best of our circumstances. Not rely on dreaming and wishing things were different. This match will give lots of publicity to our plight."

Amadeo moves towards her to hug here, but Lara recoils. From their vantage point in Amadeo's jacket pocket Skip, Rico and Loco notice this rejection and bow their heads empathetically. "Poor Amadeo. The boy not done good," Skips says, "he's had a shocker, a real mare."

"It's frustrating for him. He hasn't scored a goal for a very long time," adds Gregor. They all turn to look at him. "What? It's true. If he's going to take on Flash, he's got to hit Flash where it hurts and make the final ball in the final third count. He ain't going to have many chances against a world class defensive back four, so his strikers have got to make the few opportunities count when they come their way. Sorry, some men are just permanently obsessed with football. Real one track mind, me."

"I think we need to be more sensitive and accept that Amadeo has one other interest apart from football," suggests Loco.

"Yes, of course. How insensitive of Rico. Rico is sorry. Er… just remind Rico what that other interest is again?"

All the foosball players answer in unison: "Lara!"

"Oh yes," concedes Rico.

Skip speaks next. "I don't think we should allocate valuable resources to helping Amadeo get Lara back. OK, he likes her a lot, a real lot…"

"A real, real, real lot," interjects Loco, "which is odd because I didn't even realise girls played football."

"Lots of girls play football. Even someone made out of lead who's spent the last 40 years stuck to a rod in a café should know that," says Gregor.

"OK, we'll get Lara back," Skip says decisively. "Which team do we have to beat to accomplish that?"

"Flash's Grandmasters. The best team on the planet. An invincible side comprised of the world's greatest living players - unbeaten in ten years since Flash joined them and they haven't conceded a goal in four years. And we're taking them on at full size real soccer on a proper football pitch," Beville informs him.

His twin brother Beville Beville thinks deeply before making a statement. "That shouldn't be a problem."

The others look at him incredulously.

"What?" replies Beville. "If Amadeo's village side take on Flash's Grandmasters the referee will need an abacus. Probably two."

"They're not the only team who won't win. If Amadeo doesn't win Lara back, then you lot won't have a manager and you'll be incapable of beating any team ever again," Gregor states emphatically.

"As I was saying, we need to allocate all our resources to getting Lara back," declares Skip.

15

Lara is excited. Her face beams with the hot news she is going to enjoy sharing. Both she and Amadeo have been busy recruiting players to represent the Village Team in their forthcoming battle with Flash's Grandmasters. But getting sufficient players to agree to play has been surprisingly difficult. So far all they have collected from knocking on doors for team recruitment was a collection of "No's", "Definitely No's" and "Absolutely, irrefutably, unquestionably, irreversibly, totally 100% No's". The sound of slammed doors has provided a rhythmic backing track to all those "No's".

Lara and Amadeo have discovered a deep-seated and understandable fear among the villagers of pitting their non-existent footballing skills against Flash and the mighty reputation of his all-conquering Grandmasters: a team assembled by a billionaire Russian oligarch and staffed by footballing royalty rumoured to be on £1m-a-month contracts. Hence it is good news worthy of a big announcement when a willing recruit has been signed up to don the green and yellow stripes of the Village Team and take on The Grandmasters.

"Amadeo, I've got another player. The Village Team now has a goalkeeper." She opens the door, revealing her brother Chester who is standing there polishing an apple on his shirt.

"Ta dah!" says Chester, announcing himself. But the act of striking a pose causes him to lose his balance and he falls over with slapstick effect. His spilt apple rolls to Amadeo who gently lobs it back to him. Chester drops the apple.

"He's our star goalie," announces Lara with a slightly detectable wobble in her suddenly dented positivity.

Not to be outdone, or underdone, Amadeo also has news on the recruitment front. "Well, I've signed ourselves a midfield playmaker."

"Really?" enthuses Lara, "where?"

"At the village police station. I got our local copper to play for us, PC Robin Banks."

"Isn't the village policeman too strict? Remember he arrested our first choice goalkeeper, Gordon Banksy, for doing street art," cautions Lara.

"Yeah, he feels a bit guilty about that so he's agreed to play for us himself and let us have Fast Fingers Flynn a.k.a. the Pickpocket as a roving midfielder. He's got a terrific turn of speed, and is accomplished at getting away from his marker."

When it comes to the ignoble art of pickpocketing, there is no one faster or more accomplished than Fast Fingers Flynn a.k.a. the Pickpocket. When Amadeo signed him up for the team, he lost his pen in the process. And wallet, which the policeman ensured was dutifully returned.

"I see him more on the wing," says Amadeo.

"On E-Wing - at the prison?" Lara retorts.

"But the policeman said the Pickpocket's going nowhere as he has to watch him all the time. Until I suggested: 'Well, you could watch him on the pitch closer than his marker.' And the policeman agreed. So he's playing for us too."

Keen to top this rather unspectacular news, Amadeo reveals a further recruit he has made to the Village Team. "Plus I went to church today."

"Good managerial tactic. God on our side would be more useful than another defensive midfielder."

Earlier Amadeo has been to visit village priest Father Dick Dawkins in his confessional box. The priest greets Amadeo warmly. "Hello Amadeo. Have you being having more 'long thinks' about Lara?"

"No, Father. I need a decent midfielder for Saturday and I need the hand of God." "And I assume Maradona was unavailable?" replies Father Dick.

"Wow, you got the priest to play. Even though he's like 60 years old?" asks Lara.

"That's not true and you know it! He's only 59," counters Amadeo. "Then I thought if we've asked everyone in the village to play for us and we still need another player, there must be someone we have not yet asked. Then I remembered the Hermit.

"What, you mean Pongo Stinky Stinkman? But he's a tramp."

"No, he's a hermit. A hermit is a tramp with better PR."

Lara is amazed that Amadeo has persuaded him to join the team. "How did you recruit the famously withdrawn Hermit?"

Initially the Hermit has indeed declined. When asked to play he rebukes Amadeo by saying: "No way. I'm a hermit, I don't like people, so I can't be involved with a team that attracts a local crowd. That's why I follow Manchester United - all the fans live so far away."

Fortunately Amadeo has prepared for the Hermit's lack of social interaction by formulating a counter-argument. "Haven't you heard? Flash has knocked down the café and built a super stadium. He's also demolished the off-licence."

The Hermit suddenly starts trembling and vibrating with a mixture of distress and rage. "The café and off-licence gone! Argh! Argh! Aaaarrrgggghhhhh...NOOOOOO!!!!"

A cloud of bats flies out of the cave where the Hermit dwells high above the village. "OK, I'm in. I'll do anything to beat Flash and get the café and off-licence back. Mainly the off-licence, to be honest. Where do I sign?"

Amadeo is unsure what Lara's reaction will be to his recent recruits to the team.

"Well, they're not top of Real Madrid's or Bayern Munich's wish list. But at least we have ten players at last," Lara concedes with a traceable "I'm-making-the-best-of-it" tone in her voice. "An eleventh player would be good too."

"We need to get them organised and trained - that's the key," announces Amadeo in a voice so upbeat that it nearly persuades him that it's true.

16

Amadeo enters the makeshift dressing room at the village's training ground - a piece of scrub land with a tiny pavilion. Ironically it is the same humble environment where Flash first learned to play football. Amadeo is here to conduct a training session with his new recruits - exhibiting different levels of enthusiasm - for the Village Team. He has arrived early to decide on tactics and has brought the tiny foosballers along to talk strategies. They are all staring pensively at a whiteboard.

Amadeo pins his players' photos to a whiteboard, which only highlights the unavoidable fact they have ten players rather than the required eleven - like the blank white space left in the album of an otherwise completed football-sticker collection.

"I'll just check my emails to see if anyone else has replied to my request for villagers to play for us… hmm that's a no… another no… oh that's just rude, he could have just said 'no thank you'… no, no, no I don't want to give any money to a Nigerian princess with $10 million to invest…. Oh here's a volunteer. Gill Etre will play!"

"Er, isn't she a…?" begins Skip.

"Yes?"

"Nothing."

"Right, tactics, lads. I don't know whether to play a four-four-two formation or four-three-three."

"How about a five-four-six formation and hope the ref doesn't notice we're fielding fifteen players?" Rico roars with laughter at his own joke. He remains so debilitated by laughter, that even ten seconds later he is only capable of expressing sentences with gaps between each word to regain his composure: "Rico… is… such… a… very… funny… guy."

Everyone else in the locker room is so intent on laughing at Rico's joke, probably as a way of defusing the obvious tension of tomorrow's showdown match with Flash and his Grandmaster all-stars, that they fail to notice the hurt reaction in Amadeo's face.

Amadeo throws down his chalk and storms towards the corner of the room.

Skip follows Amadeo and finds him sitting on a broken chair, looking morose. The captain wants to console his manager. But first he attempts to climb on a stool beside Amadeo. "Er… little help for the little guy," requests Skip. Realising that he's not going to receive the requested aid, he eventually clambers up to the top of the stool himself. "You know that famous game in history when a Scottish team once lost 36-nil?"

"What do you mean?" Amadeo asks. "Is that record under threat?"

"If we work hard, close 'em down early, maintain our shape and discipline, we could keep it down to 40-nil. 50-nil tops."

Amadeo responds not with words, but by collapsing to the ground in resignation. Skip slides down the leg of the stool like a fireman responding to a call-out. His mission is to cheer Amadeo up.

"Surely we can keep our dignity," says Skip defiantly.

"At foosball we can. Not at proper football. None of us in the Village Team are real football players. You guys can play but you're tiny. Our opponents might have aerial supremacy - oh, and tread on you."

"But we're the Stripes, we're the Unbeatables, boss," Skip maintains.

"Yeah at foosball. The Grandmasters are known as the Unbeatables too - at actual football. The sport we're going to play against them."

Through the open window they hear the sobbing of a distressed female. "I recognise that sound," says Amadeo.

"Really? You must be a top boyfriend," replies Gregor. Amadeo climbs out of the dressing room window and spots Lara sitting on the ground with her back leaning up against the pavilion wall. She is crying and going through tissues at an alarming rate. Amadeo wants to comfort her. Skip clambers up onto a nearby ledge, peeking through the dressing room window.

"Amadeo?" Lara greets him, surprised to see him here.

"What's wrong?" asks Amadeo.

Lara is dismissive. "Oh, nothing. See you around." But secretly she hopes just the right amount of dismissiveness has been selected as she does not want Amadeo to go away.

"But you're crying," observes Amadeo perceptively.

Psy Kick appears at the open window next to Skip and calls out: "Hey Amadeo, Lara is crying. I think she is upset."

"Oh, well if there's nothing wrong…" begins Amadeo.

"Yes of course there's something wrong! Men: emotionally clueless. Same old story," Lara snaps.

Loco has joined Skip and Psy Kick as observers too, and imparts more wisdom. "Men are emotionally clueless. Yet footballers are emotionally incontinent. Ask any referee."

"I'm so sorry, Lara," says Amadeo with his head bowed down almost like it is at half-mast.

She pauses before remarking, "No, I'm the one who should be sorry, Amadeo, it's all my fault this is happening."

"What do you mean?"

"This. All this. Look around you. Our threatened future. The café. The village. The challenge."

"What about the challenge, Lara?"

"What about it? It's going to be like Barcelona against a non-league side with an injury crisis. It'll be as one-sided as a public hanging."

This is not the sort of pre-match encouragement Amadeo wants his team to hear. He gestures at Skip, Psy Kick and Loco to close the dressing room window in case any of Lara's words reach the Village players inside, but they just wave back at him, misunderstanding his signal as a friendly wave.

"Hey, Lara. Come on! You've got to have faith. OK, so Flash may be more famous than me," says Amadeo, stating the obvious.

"And a better passer, header, tackler, finisher, runner and tactician," says Lara.

"Yes," accepts Amadeo keen to move on… "and a better ball controller and far superior at dead-ball situations," Lara adds, " oh and he's much faster than you, and reads the game better, and has such vision on the field, and is so much more skilful and fitter," she continues, "oh sorry. Your kit colours are nicer than his."

"OK, OK…"

"They are. Really - I'm not just saying that. Your green and yellow stripes are much nicer than The Grandmasters' ugly all black kit. You can be very proud of that achievement."

"Alright. But didn't you see us in training?"

Lara shakes her head.

"Oh, you didn't see us train today. Then that's why you're upset. The team has fantastic movement off the ball. They'll be completely amazing, I'm sure."

"But," Lara points out, "you're not real football players. Plus it's likely the Grandmasters plan to use a ball in the match. That's the sort of underhand sneaky tactics I wouldn't put past them."

"They've got nothing to play for. They're just international mercenaries. But for us it's our village's entire future that's at stake," Amadeo counters.

For the first time a slightly hopeful expression starts to appear on Lara's face, like the sun determined to peak through on an overcast day. She is beginning to look as if she wants to believe him.

"We'll win. Have some faith. Seeing is believing. We're even ready to introduce a ball to tonight's training session. That's two days ahead of schedule."

They are both looking into each other's eyes. Their heads slowly move closer together. A longing surges inside Amadeo. He stands before Lara, utterly conquered by her beauty. "Wow," he thinks, "there's nothing in nature as beautiful as Lara's face.

Rainbows, shooting stars, sunsets, giraffes - all fine efforts, God, but nowhere near as beautiful as Lara." Every atom in his body is craving her touch.

They are just about to kiss when… "NOOO!!! YOU DON'T PUT IT THERE YOU STUPID MAN. IT DOESN'T GO THERE!"

"Eh?" asks Amadeo.

The kiss never comes. They are stopped midway by the Agent who is organising the testing of new floodlights installed across the road at the new Astro Dome stadium.

The Agent is speaking into the PA, his insistent mid-Atlantic brogue echoing around the stadium of empty seats. "OK. Now test the next block of lights. No. No. No. the other set of lights!"

There is a loud banging sound - then the sound of another bank of lights being switched on. Lara and Amadeo sit close together in front of the wall.

"OK, switch them all on," instructs the Agent.

Lara gets up to leave, her mood of despondency from a few minutes earlier replaced with quiet optimism. "I'll see you tomorrow, Amadeo."

The Agent continues to talk into the microphone, unwittingly broadcast throughout the stadium. "How do I turn this microphone off? Oh, is it this button? Yes, that must have been the 'off' button. These floodlights will enable the TV watching public to witness a massacre tomorrow. Ha ha ha haaaaa… ouch. Doing an evil laugh really hurts your throat."

Lara starts to walk away. After a few paces she stops in frozen motionlessness, suddenly transfixed like a distracted squirrel. She turns back. And walks towards Amadeo.

"Oh, this looks interesting," says Skip. "Interesting." Lara kisses Amadeo on the cheek, and then quickly scurries away. "Very interesting!" repeats Skip, adopting the intonation of a football commentator. "Look at his face! Just look at his face!"

Amadeo's face is beaming like a beacon on a moonless night.

He almost faints, sliding down the pavilion wall to the ground. He sits, his face glowing incandescently with affection for Lara. Cupid has clearly picked an arrow out of his quiver and shot it straight at Amadeo.

Amadeo looks up at the stars, his face ecstatic. Skip waits for Lara to walk away, a spring noticeably returned to her step, before re-joining Amadeo. "I never saw anyone so in control of their game like that," Skip informs Amadeo.

"Thanks. Was I really that good?"

"No. I don't mean you."

17

It's match day. The Agent has ensured that the game has received blanket media coverage. Every news outlet throughout the solar system appears to be covering it.

Lara makes her way to the stadium, loyally adorned in a green and yellow striped shirt to show her support for the Village Team. She passes a football pundit doing a live pre-match piece to camera: "It's Judgement Day. Only bigger!"

With kick-off rapidly approaching the Agent is giving a final briefing to assembled TV producers in the new stadium's huge media suite. "Remember, lots of close-ups on my boy Flash. You… whatever your name is… I said I wanted a double shot espresso with skinny soya milk stirred anti clockwise; this is clearly a double shot espresso with skinny soya milk stirred clockwise. And bring me a biscuit, oh and your resignation letter. QUICKLY!"

That feels good, the Agent thinks. He had been so busy with match day preparations and brokering media deals that he has completely forgotten to sack anyone today until now.

Meanwhile Amadeo is also trying to conduct a last minute briefing. "Chester, don't forget your goalkeeping gloves!" He throws them at Chester, who fails to react until they have already hit the floor. "On second thoughts, you probably won't be needing them much this afternoon," concludes Amadeo. "Right, we're operating a flat back ten. Who wants to play at the back?" All the Village Team, except Pongo Stinky "the Hermit" Stinkman raise their hands. "OK, we'll operate with a back nine, leaving Pongo in characteristic isolation all on his own upfront."

"Good tactics, boss," whispers Skip into his ear. Skip and Rico are positioned like a concealed mouthpiece, hiding in his jacket lapel. "Be prepared to soak up a lot of pressure."

"Rico thinks it will be like soaking up the ocean and you only have one small sponge. Then, we'll hit them on the break. Or, preferably during the break, whilst they're having a half-time cuppa. OK, Rico maybe not helping now."

Amadeo's mood becomes suddenly serious. "Today, men… sorry, and Gill… we have something true men… and Gill… rarely hold in their own hands. That is an ability to create their destiny. Not discover it, or react to it, or receive it - but to actually shape it ourselves. What we achieve on that football pitch in the next 90 minutes will shape our lives, our village, our destiny. So I say unto you: once more unto the breach, dear friends, once more… No Chester, I said 'the breach'… we're not going to the beach."

The momentousness of the occasion begins to seep into the players. Noise from the huge crowd permeates through the thick concrete dressing room walls. An official knocks on the door. "Time to line up in the tunnel," he orders.

Amadeo uses the only remaining seconds he has with his team to issue his final words of motivation before his eleven players cross that white line: "Right, everybody. You've all got a village to save."

18

A roar greets the players as both teams enter the pitch. The noise is so loud it feels like the stadium roof is about to be lifted free of its shackling pillars.

Television commentators Bob and Ray are in the gantry describing the scene. "And that's the unbelievable atmosphere greeting the teams for the first ever game at the world's newest and biggest stadium, the Astro Dome. Specially built to contain the giants of soccer and even bigger giant ego of world supremo Flash, megastar of the all-conquering global superstars the Grandmasters versus, er, the local village team."

Amadeo is nervously caressing a ball, looking out from the pitch at the vast crowd. Spectators' cameras are blinking and flickering. Thousands of hands applaud as if the stadium is full of tiny butterflies. He knows he should be drinking in this experience, sipping not gulping, to relish it - but it is making his stomach ache with nerves. Skip and Rico are standing next to him, side by side - literally and figuratively. All the players, full-sized and foosballers, are wearing the same green and yellow striped kit.

"Don't worry, boss. The nerves will go once the whistle blows," says Skip encouragingly.

Above the commentators in the gantry the Agent issues more orders: "Come on, introduce the teams. His Stroppiness is getting impatient. There's only one name that matters here. Flash."

The camera pans along the Grandmasters team, tight black jerseys struggling to contain their Adonis-framed muscles. Commentator Bob speaks into his microphone: "And here they are, footy fans. The Grandmasters who have put out their top strength team today. Legends to a man. First up its former Arsenal superstar defender... Don Keyes, then Dutchman Patrik van der Wacky-Bak, the German Herr Kutt, then 4. Pete Sake, Wee Jocky MacSporran - much capped by Wales, Argentinian Mani Balas, 7. Ed Lee Syns and stroppy French genius Sacramerd. The man between the sticks is Saf Hans - his girlfriend says he's a keeper. Then Englishman Phil Kettle. And the world's greatest player... Vince 'Flash' Butpane!

"Plus there's real international quality on the bench today for the Grandmasters. Their permitted substitutes are: Moroccan Mustafa Penref, the German defender Herr Dreyer, Brazilian Shaun Vaggio and Swede defender Borg Ikea, an advocate of the Swedish flat-pack four system. And we haven't got time to list the wealth of extensive talent on the bench - we'll namecheck the remaining Grandmasters substitutes later as I understand some breaking team selection news is coming through, Bob..."

"And we're just hearing that the Village Team are not naming any substitutes as they failed to recruit more than eleven players. Apparently their one named substitute couldn't make it due to a children's birthday party but is 'hopeful of maybe popping in for the last ten minutes of the match depending on the traffic'. You've got to say the Grandmasters are the more professional of the outfits on display here today, Ray."

"They certainly are, Bob," replies Ray.

"And today's referee is top Italian official Signor Bunga. Often requires an escort off the pitch. And his assistants are also Italian: Ricardo Yelocardo and Flaggio 'The Bat' Pipistrello."

Looking physically dwarfed by the Grandmasters, the distinctly un-athletic silhouettes of the Village Team appear into view on the television screens. One of them, Spencer, is smoking a pre-match cigarette. Moxey clumsily hides a pipe behind his back as the camera pans along the line.

Commentator Bob announces the players as they appear on his monitor. "And here they are: the Village Team. First up parish priest Father Dick Dawkins, then pub pools syndicate organiser Spencer next to his psychic side-kick pools predictor Moxey.

Pickpocket and speed merchant Fast Fingers Flynn. Goalkeeper Chester Dropbit - gloves sponsored by Meadowfarm Butter. Tristan Tarquin Smythe, known as 'The Emo Kid'. Policeman Robin Banks. He'll take no prisoners today."

"That's 'cos he's off-duty today, Bob," interjects co-commentator Ray. "Next up is Ewan Whosarmy known simply as the Guv'nor." "Unlikely to feel a piano dropped on him from a 9th storey window," observes Ray. "Isolated all on his own up front is Pongo Stinky 'the Hermit' Stinkman."

"Expect he'll be making a B-O-line for goal, Bob."

"Then a surprise selection in the village team, the hirsute Gill Etre."

"And finally Village Team captain and player-manager Amadeo." Amadeo holds up to the camera a homemade sign advertising: "Watch live football. It's really good. If you like that sort of thing."

"And that's a very poor advert for the game, Ray."

"It certainly is, Bob. This is not the occasion for advertising."

"That's right, Ray. And before we can kick off, I must

thank today's match sponsors: FedUpEx, the village's no. 1 deliverer of divorce settlements. Tsarbucks - the village's Russian coffee shop. The village's pet grooming parlour Doggie Style. Spudweiser - the King Edward of beers. Tea-Mobile - Fat Barry's tea and butty van. HP Sauce - buy now, pay later. And why not dine out at the village's French restaurant Horses For Courses? Or purchase from Poundstretcher – as their name implies - stretchers for one pound. Popular brand PG Strips offer DVDs rated PG of strippers removing coats, hats, scarves and gloves only.

"Or stay at the Village's YMCA (sorry no builders, policemen, cowboys or chiefs permitted). And our coverage of today's game is brought to you in association with our official broadcast partners… can you read them out, Ray?"

"OK Bob, but I've forgotten my reading glasses. Our sponsors are: Brutish Telecom, The Royal Sank of Botchland, Merrill Lynchmob, Stalkers Crisps, DisasterCard, PowerGen Italia, Tacky Bell, Vodaphonies, L'Ordeal, Thai Poo Tea, Merdes-Bents, Premier Din Hotels, Apple Cack, Café Dearo, Killerlogs All Bran, Blackberry Crumble, Pedigree Bum, Proctology Gamble, Carmoan Swearspouse, General Floaters and Nikeit - 'just nick it'."

"Thanks, Ray - masterfully done."

Both sides prepare for kick off. Flash is looking arrogant and eerily confident, like a cat about to snack on a helpless mouse. Amadeo and his Village Team are visibly shaking with trepidation.

Amadeo has smuggled in all the foosballers in his kit bag and positioned them underneath the unoccupied home bench, their heads protruding above the blades of grass like meadow flowers. Gregor crosses himself. Skip asks him what he is doing. "No idea," replies Gregor, "but everyone does it. Check wallet, phone, keys?" "And we're ready to start. This is the big one, isn't it, Ray?"

"Sure is Bob. It's Judgement Day. Only bigger."

"That's right, Ray. And now sports fans, it's time to buckle yourself in for some non- stop action. It's the Grandmasters v. The Village live and exclusive on this channel. Here we're…"

"The provider for the decider."

"Putting the rumpus on your compass." "Bringing the tension to your attention." "Showing High Noon in the afternoon."

"With the facilities to cover hostilities," "The focus on the commocus." "Don't think that last one's actually a word, Ray."

"Pheep!" The referee's whistle starts play. Or at least it is supposed to. Amadeo and Gill Etre are standing on the centre-spot, but appear remarkably reluctant to commence proceedings by kicking-off. "Pheeeeeeep!" goes the official's whistle again, this time noticeably more impatient. "Come on, kick the ball!" orders the ref.

"And Signor Bunga is showing Gill Etre a yellow card for time wasting in the opening six seconds."

"Technically in the opening zero second, Bob, as we haven't kicked off yet."

Eventually the game gets underway. Gill Etre passes the ball behind her to Spencer who slides it backwards to Moxey. Moxey looks at the ball like it is a hitherto unseen item from outer space that has just landed on his lawn. He is reluctant to go anywhere near it.

"Pass it, my child!" shouts Father Dick Dawkins. But Fast Fingers Flynn nicks it from Spencer and starts an attack.

Commentator Bob describes the scene. "Spencer passes it to Moxey on the overlap out on the left wing where the Priest is screaming for the ball." The home crowd are nervous, wanting for the Priest to pass the ball. But his distribution is good and he crosses to Amadeo in central midfield, only for the Grandmasters to intercept easily. Bob's voice rises in energy in the commentary box: "The Grandmasters have options here, and play switches out to Dutchman Van der Wacky-Bak in so much space he has time for a fag break before passing to No. 4 Pete Sake in the middle of the park."

The Grandmasters pass the ball around effortlessly, comfortably controlling possession. A deft flick finds Englishman Phil Kettle on the right whose neat first time lay-off invites Sacramerd to shoot.

"The Frenchman's shot rockets off the underside of the bar and out to safety."

"The goal frame is still vibrating several seconds later, Bob."

Fortuitously the ball rebounds to a Village Team defender who instinctively hoofs it upfield. At that very moment goalkeeper Chester begins his woefully late dive. "And after a bright start, the home team are beginning to look slower than an aging sloth with some heavy shopping," chips in commentator Ray.

The visitors surge forward again, fizzing the ball around the park. "I've seen warehouse complexes with less space than the Grandmasters' midfielders are currently enjoying."

"Welsh wizardry from Wee Jockie McSporran finds Flash in acres of space."

"Make that hectares of space, Bob"

"And his shot is deflected by a courageous last-ditch block by the Village's Emo Kid."

The ball flies up in the air and down towards Chester, the Village Team's goalkeeper. Such is the fierce velocity of Flash's shot that the ball rockets high into the air. Chester decides to take control of the situation, especially as the ball is dropping with menacing speed towards his goal: "I've got it. I've got it. I've got it. I've got it. I've got it. I've got it. I've got it. I've got it."

Bob continues describing the action: "The ball is hanging in the air. The keeper's coming for it… but Flash pops up like just ready toast at the near post, and heads home."

GOOOAAALLLL!!! The crowd roars its approval.

"I haven't got it," concludes Chester. "The keeper hasn't got it," commentates Bob. "He hasn't got it," announces Psy Kick.

The stadium scoreboard displays Village 0 Grandmasters 1.

The scoreboard operator decides against walking back to his seat and remains next to the board - he is expecting to change it again very soon.

"And you've got to say, Ray, it's all too easy for the Grandmasters."

Skip, Rico, Loco, Gregor, Psy Kick and Mac stand on the bench in shock. Mac the Keeper looks especially bemused at the non-goalkeeping antics he has just witnessed. Lara, sitting in the stands, is equally shaken while the crowd around her celebrates. Lara forgets to close her mouth she is so shocked. A swear word sneaks out of her usually sophisticated mouth.

"The Village keeper looked more uncomfortable at the sight of a cross than most vampires, Bob," observes Ray. "Less than two minutes on the clock and the Village Team are left with a mountain to climb. And I mean Everest in bad weather without sherpas or oxygen."

Flash takes the applause, his arms held out in celebration, beckoning the adulation towards him. Amadeo retrieves the ball from the net.

"Come on, guys. We can still do it. We've still got eighty-eight minutes and thirty-nine seconds to play. Approximately."

Amadeo kicks off again.

The visitors continue where they left off - on the attack. "Lovely stuff from the Grandmasters," says Bob approvingly. Flash traps the ball on his heel, flicks it over his head and beguiles the Guv'nor with a couple of step-overs before dragging the ball back and beating his opponent for speed.

"More fantastic trickery and wing wizardry from Flash there. He'll soon be asking his man-marker 'to pick a card, any card' he's so full of tricks."

"Not sure if the home side realise the ball is an essential part of the game, Bob."

Again the Grandmasters appear unstoppable as another attack surges towards the Village goal. After superb approach work from the black-shirted Grandmasters, Pete Sake drills the ball low towards the target. It bounces off the underside of the bar. The crowd gasp while Chester tries to pounce onto the rebounding ball. Amadeo immediately runs in to help.

"The home keeper is stranded and flapping like a salmon on a river bank."

Chester is clutching the ball to his chest and won't move.

"Chester, what are you doing?" Amadeo enquires

"I'm time-wasting."

"But we're losing."

"Yes, but only by one goal," replies Chester, "result, eh?"

On the touchline, Skip is going mad. "They're not listening. All week I've trained them, discussed tactics with Amadeo, formulated a game plan, and they're ignoring everything I said."

"What was the formulated game plan?" asks Gregor

"Not turning up for the match."

Eventually Amadeo prises the ball from Chester's clutched hands and the game restarts. Commentator Bob takes up the action: "The Village Team on a rare foray into the Grandmasters' half are on the attack with the Guv'nor hitting a long ball to Amadeo. Beautiful pass, oh, but Flash has stolen it from Amadeo."

"First I steal your girlfriend, and now your ball, ha ha," Flash sneers at Amadeo as he robs him of possession. He then dribbles the ball around the Village Team's defenders, as though they were stationary cones in a training session.

"The Village's defence couldn't locate Flash with sniffer dogs, Bob."

Flash lays off the ball and continues his run, sneaking into the penalty area with an assassin's stealth. His run culminates in receiving the return pass. He shimmies around another bamboozled Village defender and unleashes a vicious goalbound shot.

As the ball flies past him into the goal, Chester stands rooted to the spot thinking "the ball should be coming into view soon… any second now I should be seeing the shot… in just a moment the ball should appear in my line of vision…" unaware that the net has swished and swayed several seconds earlier.

The stadium explodes with the collective word: "GOOAAALLL!!!"

The frightening propulsion of Flash's missile means the scoreboard now reads: Village 0 Grandmasters 2.

"Chester, Moxey has already retrieved the ball from the back of the net. Can't you hear the crowd celebrating the goal?" Amadeo asks.

But like a bullet it was too fast for Chester to see with the naked eye. Also difficult to see with the naked eye are the tiny figures amassed underneath the vacant Village Team's bench. Loco, Rico, Skip, Gregor, Mac and Psy Kick look dismayed.

"Why are the crowd cheering? They should be booing the baddies, not cheering them," ponders Rico.

"Travel is the journey not the destination. The crowd believe the Grandmasters are first class and we are cargo economy class. They have upgraded themselves by supporting the aristocrats," says Loco, somewhat opaquely.

"He means footy fans are fickle and like to be associated with a winning side," clarifies Gregor.

"The Village are losing 2-nil." Says Psy Kick. "I think the Village Team will lose this match."

"Psy Kick really is psychic, isn't he? And annoying," adds Rico.

Back on the pitch Flash smiles cruelly, before turning to a hapless Amadeo and sneering, "2-0 already, Loser! I'm going to personally demolish your house. Sure, it's more cost efficient if I let the bulldozer crew demolish it with the rest of your stinky village in one job, but the pleasure of destroying your house myself is... well, that'll certainly be one of my career highlights."

Then Flash turns back to the camera and smiles sweetly.

19

Manning the screens in the control room, the director calls for more close-ups of Flash.

But the producer is concerned. Not everyone in the stadium is enjoying the football masterclass being taught by the Grandmasters. In the television technician's room the gantry is far from content. "It's too easy. The Village Team are a hopeless shower. There's no competition or sense of a contest. This is too one-sided," complains one assistant director to another. "That's right. This lot couldn't beat a girls' team playing in high heels," agrees a producer.

The Agent speaks into Flash's earpiece. "We need to create the illusion of suspense. Leave some space for the Village to play, make it look like it's a proper contest. Just spray the ball around a bit, do some of your fancy tricks."

Flash is mystified. "Why? You know I detest two things: arrogance and showing-off."

"Er... right. Really? Of course, Flash. But we need to create more of a show for the TV audience."

"No. I want to destroy the Village, inflict such a humiliation on them that all eleven of their so-called players will be phobic about ever playing football again. I'll make them squirm."

But the Agent insists: "Remember, Flash, it's money not revenge that makes the world go round."

"I want to obliterate them. I plan to inflict a defeat on them so harrowing they're never be able to play football again without enduring decades of counselling first."

"They're be time for that near the end of the game, Flash.

At the moment just show-off your skills and fancy footwork, do some showboating. Keep the scoreline at 2-nil until half time to create the illusion the Village Team can still get back into this game. It'll keep the TV viewers watching, and create a bigger audience to adulate you in the second-half."

Meanwhile, back on the pitch Flash revels in his centre-stage ability to perform tricks, flicks and kicks. Selfishly monopolising the ball, the Grandmasters' captain treats the crowd to his skills.

"At the end of the day it's 11.59 pm, Ray," announces Bob the commentator.

"And we predicted pre-match this day would end with the Village Team tasting the bitterest taste of defeat - a taste no amount of brushing with any amount of toothpaste can eradicate."

"That's right, Bob. They're simply isn't that much mouthwash commercially available."

"Er, thanks, Ray," says a slightly bewildered Bob. "We're certainly high in the gantry here."

So far the tiny foosballer players standing underneath what looks to the TV viewing public at home like a vacant Village bench, are not enjoying the game at all. "The last time I saw this much one-way traffic I was…" Skip says before pausing, wondering how to finish his sentence.

"… standing at the side of a one way street?" Gregor offers.

"Er, yeah… that'll do. My point here is…"

"Never start an analogy you cannot finish?" suggests Gregor.

"Saying that's comparable to…er…um… Why don't you shut up, Pinkman?"

"It's Claret. Are you colour blind as well as stupid?" Gregor snarls.

"Guys, this attitude makes Loco very sad. My own brothers, my own flesh and blood… my own lead and paint… We should not be fighting. We need to think of ways to stop seeing this terrible humiliation befalling Amadeo. So I've decided…

"… yes?" ask his team mates with heightened curiosity.
"I've decided to turn my back on the game."
"How is that helping?" asks Skip.

20

Signor Bunga draws a deep breath that he immediately exhales to signal three "Pheep-Pheep-Pheeeeeeep" notes on his whistle. The stadium scoreboard displays: "Half time: Village 0 Grandmasters 2". "That's half time," announces Psy Kick, "the Village are 2-nil down."

"The boy Amadeo done great," says Mac the Keeper.

"But not in his grammar or elocution class," notes Loco.

"They've done superb," continues Mac the Keeper, "to keep the deficit down to only 2-nil at the break, don't yer think?"

"Yes," agrees Loco, "but don't yer think the Village side literally not touching the ball for the last 30 minutes of the first half is an ominous sign?"

"Come on guys, let's go to the dressing room to hear the half time team-talk," suggests Skip.

"And how are we going to get into the dressing room?" asks Gregor.

"Easy. Everybody jump into Amadeo's trainer's bag at the side of the bench here and he'll carry us there." The players, both Stripes and Clarets, enthusiastically commence climbing into Amadeo's capacious bag. "Wait, no one gives my team orders," states Gregor. "Right, everyone jump into Amadeo's bag and he'll carry us there."

Amadeo comes over to the Village bench and collects his trainer's bag. The Village side then trundle dejectedly towards the Home dressing room, passing Flash giving a TV interview in the tunnel. "Yes, thank you. I was rather magnificent, wasn't I? Of course, that was just a technical training session. In the second half I will be demonstrating my finishing skills. So stay tuned for a goal avalanche in the second half of the match... sorry, did I say 'the match'? I meant, of course, 'the rout'!"

Sitting in glum despondency, too morose and disheartened to speak, the Village Team ignore the half-time oranges and tea in their dressing room. Eventually Chester breaks the doleful silence: "Throw me an orange, Amadeo."

"Actually... if you don't mind... I'd prefer to pass you one rather than throw it. I'd also bring you over a tea, but fear you'll spill that too." It is the lone exchange of words uttered in ten minutes of awkward silence.

Hidden in the trainer's bag Skip is growing uneasy. "Amadeo should be using this valuable time to lead and motivate them!"

"Words... um... ah... no... err..." begins Gregor.

"Fail you?" adds Skip.

"Words are needed. Definitely needed," says Gregor. "Skip is actually right. I know, I know... by simple law of averages it had to happen eventually. Amadeo needs to say something. To inspire his men or they'll just capitulate in the second half. Even more than they capitulated in the first half."

An official knocks on the Village Team's door. "You have three minutes." They are fully intent on spending those final two minutes in steadfast mute uncommunicativeness, but there is another knock on the dressing room door.

"Yeah, OK, we're coming in three minutes," says Amadeo. "Though I honestly can't see the point."

"Are you decent? Well, not at football, obviously - I mean are you all dressed?" It is a female voice and one that Amadeo recognises as quickly as he is surprised to hear it.

"Lara?" he says, his voice unsteady with shock.

"Please may I come in for one minute?"

"Yes, of course. Come in, Lara. But we have to be in the tunnel in two minutes for the second half - unless we just attach one of these white towels to a corner flag and surrender."

Lara laughs sweetly, and Amadeo discovers himself feeling a surge of affection for her. She speaks in a calm and soft voice. "I'm so sorry to trouble you, but… and only if you consider it appropriate… please may I address the team and perhaps say a few brief words?"

"Of course," says Amadeo.

Suddenly Lara's voice, demeanour and personality are transformed. She yells like the scariest headmistress ever: "Call yourself a team?! YOU LOT ARE PATHETIC! That's right, there's a woman doing your half time team talk, and yet surely my pretty little head isn't sophisticated enough to understand the offside rule… which apparently depends on the ability to count to two. Yeah, women are capable of being Prime Ministers and astronauts, but the offside rule will always remain too complex for our comprehension", she shouts, becoming even more furious.

Inside Amadeo's bag Psy Kick remarks: "I think she is being sarcastic. She is also angry."

"So I cannot understand the offside rule," continues Lara getting, if anything, even angrier, "or why you're the biggest bunch of losers ever to inhabit Loserville, county town of Losershire, capital of Loserland!"

Roused by Lara's speech, the foosballers collectively risk popping their heads above the zip line of Amadeo's bag. Just in time to experience the full volume of Lara's larynx yelling… "You. Are. A. Disgrace."

Rico protectively grabs his hair as if it was a wig in danger of being blown backwards from Lara's hairdryer treatment. Meanwhile Loco's dreadlocks are flowing behind his head, like a motorcyclist's scarf.

"You lot are a disgrace to football, to the team, to the village, to the human race…to the toy industry."

The foosballers, concerned they have been spotted at this stage, dip their heads down into the bag.

"Oh, you've dropped your towel," remarks Lara to one of

the Village Team who has accidently let go of the towel during the rollicking. "Don't worry, it's nothing I haven't seen before - playing for the Village in that first half!"

A crack now starts to appear in the dressing room wall due to the intensity of the boisterous bollocking.

"The four corner flags were more mobile in the first half than this back four. The midfield were like honest politicians i.e. utterly non-existent, and the keeper couldn't catch a bus. And as for the strikers' finishing abilities, not only couldn't you hit a cow's arse with a banjo, you're incapable of hitting an elephant's backside with a double bass. I've seen sloths with rigor mortis that move faster than you lot."

Light bulbs shatter, another crack appears in the plasterwork, and a passing fly vaporises in front of Lara's yelling mouth. She then unleashes a hail of expletives. If her team-talk was being broadcast, the required number of bleeps would give the impression her speech was in Morse code: "For [bleep] sake, you [bleep] [bleep] [bleep] and [bleep] and hopeless [bleep] [bleep] [bleeping] [bleeps]."

"You're play isn't just lacking an end product, it's lacking a beginning and middle product too. You're being outplayed, outthought, outmanoeuvred, outfoxed, outwitted and outclassed."

"Over 150 years of The Beautiful Game, instantly transformed into The Ugly Game by you lot of duffers, cloggers and space-wasting no-hopers in only 45 minutes. You're not just getting the hair dryer treatment," she snarls while tipping out the contents of her bag onto the treatment table, "but I've brought my hot curling tongs and heated hair straighteners."

The Village Team look even more worried, pressing themselves further back against the dressing room's tiled wall.

"These bad boys reach temperatures of 220 degrees centigrade. And I'm plugging them in now to brand your slow backsides with the word 'loser'. Unless you turn this game around in the second half!"

Cautiously, the foosballers risk another view of the half time rollicking and pop their heads up out of the bag again like twenty-two curious resurfacing moles.

"I want the opposition's midfield closed down quicker than a High Street in a recession. I want you to work so hard that footballers' legs falling off due to over-exertion becomes a recognisable medical condition and syndrome after this match," she bawls.

"Remember I'm friends with most of your wives and girlfriends in this village, so if you don't score in this next 45 minutes, expect that situation to continue pretty much indefinitely at home. So get out there and turn this around. Work, work, work and work!

"Right, I'm now so delirious with anger I appear to be hallucinating and seeing twenty-two tiny little men in the room." Another Village player drops his towel. "Make that twenty-three."

Whereas the Village Team moped into the dressing room at half time, they now depart galvanised with purposeful intention, their studs clattering on the tunnel's concrete floor as they head towards the pitch. They are relishing the resumption of hostilities against Flash's Grandmasters in the second half.

Lara then speaks privately to Amadeo, whispering into his ear: "It's completely up to you, Amadeo, but if you ever want to see me again, you'll need to find a way of winning this game."

Taken aback by Lara's comment, Amadeo leaves the dressing room without his trainer's bag. Returning to retrieve it, he spots the referee Signor Bunga chatting in the tunnel with the Agent. Both men are looking devoutly unprincipled. The Agent hands the referee a fat envelope. "Here's a little gift for your… hmm… err… forthcoming wedding," he says. He offers the ref his most golden smile, before whistling the tune "Here Comes the Bride". "I recognise that tune," says a passing Amadeo, "isn't it 'Here Comes the Bribe'?"

21

"And with the second period about to start," commentates Bob, "the Village appear to be sticking with an unchanged line-up."

"Looks like they're determined to stick with their first half game plan of abject failure, Bob."

"Quite frankly the Village Team appeared knackered from the opening minute in that first half, and looked like a side of randomly assembled people who have never played football before."

"That's true Bob, probably because they are a side of randomly assembled people who have never played football before."

"And you have to say it showed, Ray."

"And in contrast to the Village's empty subs bench, just look at the international talent on show on the Grandmasters' bench: Frenchman Jay Mangefrog, Russian Warren Peece, Scotsman Willie Puller and Chinaman Won Wei Street."

With their feelings bruised and emotions smarting from the tongue-lashing Lara has just administered, the Village kick off to start the second half like men (and one woman) with a mission. But the act of kicking-off proves to be the only possession the green and yellow striped team enjoys in the opening few minutes after the re-start - even though they are noticeably more animated and visibly pumped for the fight by Lara's rabble-rousing roasting.

Under the Village bench, the foosballers have again climbed out of Amadeo's bag but are not enjoying the direction the game is taking.

"Almost constant possession from the Grandmasters, the Village Team's contribution looks like being limited in this second-half to taking occasional throw-ins and goal-kicks," says Bob.

"And a lot of picking the ball out of their net and kicking-off," predicts Ray.

"Rico does not know defeat. He knows only triumph and applause. Rico cannot deal with this. Rico may quit football and join the theatre instead. In showbusiness there is no jealousy or backbiting. Only triumph, harmony and applause."

"Right," says Gregor, "I'm gonna roll down my socks and remove them."

"Why?" asks Mac the Keeper.

"So I can give them to Rico and tell him to put a sock in it!"

Then Loco looks like he has had an idea. A Very Good Idea: "What do you need most when the only way to win is to risk everything?"

The others look unsure.

"What do you need when the rules don't matter anymore? When deception is just another tactic for playing the game? In order to win at all costs! What do you need?"

All the foosball players look at each other and share a look of sudden realisation, shouting in joyful unison: "Passion!"

"I was going to say 'bribes'. But yeah, 'passion' is much better," says Skip.

"All is fair in love and football," promulgates Loco.

As one, as if responding to an invisible cue, the foosball players link hands and run purposefully onto the pitch. "The odds just got a lot better for the Village side," shouts Skip as a war cry entering the pitch. They cross the white line and enter the field of play, invisible to the naked eye as they part blades of grass with their arms as if hacking through dense jungle growth. Their faces, struggling to reach a few millimetres above the grass, resemble tiny daises.

From behind a blade of grass Skip watches the Grandmasters' star striker Van der Wacky-Bak moving forward, skipping around the calamitous Village defence, and just as he raises his shooting boot to arrow the ball past a cowering Chester ("not the face, not the face" pleads the hapless Village goalie), Skip, Rico and Loco jump up and grab Van der Wacky Bak's standing-foot and unbalance him - sending him thumping to the ground.

"He seems to have gone down out of nothing!" observes Bob. "For me the lad went down far too easily - like a new born foal on a frozen lake." "A contender for 'simile of the season' there, Ray."

The referee Signor Bunga is not impressed. "Yellow card there for simulation, Ray."

"Much deserved, Bob. I've seen less convincing dives in international competition from Tom Daley."

"That's right, Ray. The referee knew there was no contact given that the Village defenders haven't got within ten metres of the Grandmaster attackers all game."

From the restart the Grandmasters immediately break into a threatening position again - threatening, that is, until Ed Lee Syn's attempt to connect with a defence-splitting pass ends with another expert trip from the invisible foosballers.

Watching in the TV gantry, a puzzled expression appears on the Agent's fat face. "Why are these players falling over on their overpaid backsides?" asks the director.

Several of the Grandmasters start arguing among themselves. For the first time in the game, they appear rattled. Not for the first time, meanwhile, the Pickpocket is caught in possession - though for the first time on a football field.

"The Grandmasters are pushing forward, knocking the ball around with seemingly effortless conviction. Flash is bearing down on goal with the ball," commentates Bob. While Flash readies himself to shoot, Mac the Keeper runs over to Chester, who is setting himself ready for the shot - mainly by covering his eyes.

"Chester looks like a mouse before a swooping eagle," co-commentator Ray observes. A visibly trembling Chester shuts his eyes awaiting the potent cannon-velocity of Flash's shot. Mac climbs up Chester's leg, onwards through his shirt and resurfaces on his shoulder. At this moment Flash hits the ball sweetly and it rockets towards the top corner. Surely neither a competent keeper, nor Chester, would be able to get anywhere near a shot of this calibre. But Skip, Loco, Rico, Psy Kick and the Beville brothers have other plans. They jump onto Chester's standing leg and topple him over creating the impression he is diving towards the ball. Mac the Keeper scrambles along the length of Chester's outstretched arm and launches himself like a trapeze artist. Sailing through the air Mac tips the ball safely around the corner of the post. "What a spectacular save!" exclaims Bob, his voice full of admiration. "What a save!"

"My word, Bob. Brilliant finger-tip acrobatics from the corpulent keeper," says Ray. "Chester soared through the air like a porky comet."

From the resultant corner two Grandmasters fall over mystifyingly; the foosballers have tripped two more giants.

Flash grabs a teammate by the lapels and berates him. "You're useless. I'll going to have you replaced, do you understand? You are only here because of me. Never forget that, you worm. Now get out of my sight." Flash motions to the Grandmasters' bench to make a substitution.

Commentator Bob has spotted a detectable change in the superstars' body language. "The Grandmasters are arguing amongst themselves. The pressure has got to them. And they're bringing on a substitute."

Although Grandmaster attacks are occurring with a relentless inevitability, their expected third goal is not. A seemingly goalbound shot from Patrik van der Wacky-Bak is heroically pushed around the post by the Beville twins guarding the back stick at a corner. "And the ball appears to have a momentum all of its own there - swerving around the post at the last second in a challenge to the laws of physics governing the trajectory of moving objects, Ray."

"The boy Isaac Newton has had a shocker there, Bob, no doubt about it."

The game restarts with an intercepted goal kick that falls invitingly to a Grandmaster with time and space for a shot. But the minute foosballers ensure the ball bobbles by pushing it above the turf from underneath just as the player's boot is about to connect. The Grandmaster falls over in an undignified heap, much to the crowd's audible derision. This allows the Guv'nor time to clear the ball.

Skip and Loco are still clinging to the ball after causing its bobble. As the Guv'nor kicks it Loco crosses himself furiously. With the Guv'nor connecting with the force of a runaway coal train, the ball and its two tiny stowaways are launched skywards.

After a considerable wait the ball returns to earth. "And the astronauts would have got a good view of that clearance out of their Space Station window, Bob." Grandmasters' substitute Borg Ikea jumps for a header. But the countering momentum caused by gravity and the presence of Skip and Loco knocks him flat on the ground.

Commentator Bob is startled. "What happened there? He went down like he'd been steam-hammered into the turf." A stretcher comes onto the field and the Grandmasters substitute their substitute.

High up in the gantry, the Agent is struggling to believe it.

There is also a newly incredulous tone to commentator Bob's voice: "Incredible. The Grandmasters are fighting among themselves."

Flash grabs the dazed Borg Ikea on the stretcher. "Get up. Get up, you coward. What are you doing? Either play for me or it's a transfer back to Losers United." Meanwhile, benefitting from the invisible help of the Stripes and Clarets foosballers, the Pickpocket Fast Fingers Flynn exploits the distraction as the Grandmasters argue; he sidles over and runs off with the ball.

"And the Pickpocket has stolen the ball. That'll be going on eBay tonight. But no! He's raiding the opposition's half, hoping to perform a smash and grab raid on his illustrious opponents."

Alerted by the sound of a suddenly excited crowd, Flash sees the danger and drops his departing teammate back onto the stretcher, giving chase after the Pickpocket. But rather than turn a profit, the Pickpocket turns a defender and passes to Pongo Stinky "the Hermit" Stinkman. As the Village Team run towards the Grandmasters' goal, Gregor and Loco launch a Stripes player between them and throw him upwards, enabling him to head the ball away from a Grandmaster boot.

"What happened there? He's missed it completely?" asks a taken aback commentator Bob.

The Hermit neatly offsets the attention of two closing Grandmaster defenders by breathing on them, then passes back to the Pickpocket, who threads a through ball to the Emo Kid.

"Fast Fingers Flynn has unlocked the combination of the Grandmasters defence there," observes Bob.

The foosball players then carry the ball on their collective shoulders like leaf-carrying ants, weaving the ball through the legs of the Grandmasters' German international defensive duo Herr Kutt and Herr Dreyer. Commentator Bob is impressed. "He was sold a dummy easier than a mother with crying twins."

"Yes," agrees Ray, "that lad the Emo Kid could nutmeg a mermaid."

"Biting satire," says Bob approvingly.

The Emo Kid is through on goal. But Flash barges him aside and steals the ball, passing it back into a dangerous area deep within the Village Team's half. The Emo Kid presses both of his flat palms to the turf and raises himself up. Suddenly he is very angry, snorting outrage through his nostrils like a bull in a china shop. His mood, character and physical appearance have changed. He looks like a man who has just taken a potion.

The referee awards a free kick for the scythe on the Emo Kid and brings play back to the edge of the Grandmasters' penalty area. "First time the Village Team get near the Grandmasters' box and it's a cynical scythe," Skip tells his compadres.

Gregor is not happy with what he has just witnessed. "Surely that's more than a yellow card, referee! He was through on goal!"

"Rico believes the referee is colour blind. The referee must stop at a yellow traffic light, it is the only explanation."

The referee would undoubtedly have taken Flash's name, had the Pickpocket not stolen the official's notebook earlier.

Team captain Amadeo takes responsibility and places the ball on the edge of the penalty area-D to take the free kick himself. "Oi, get that stuff off me," shouts Skip as the referee sprays foam over the turf where the diminutive foosballer is hiding. Meanwhile Mac the Keeper cagily climbs up the goalpost and runs along the crossbar with the agility of a tiny squirrel.

Amadeo takes his time teeing up the ball, inadvertently allowing Mac to get into position on the crossbar. Mac locates himself just above the Grandmasters' international-standard keeper who is busy directing the construction of the defensive wall in front of him.

The ref strides out the regulation ten metres. A wall is formed and Saf Hans, the keeper, sets himself. "There's no doubt a goalkeeper of his quality will stop Amadeo," predicts commentator Bob confidently.

Tension is filling the stadium like a gas. Everyone is watching intently. Lara is studying Amadeo's every move.

"That's right, Bob. There's no way an amateur can score against a keeper of this pedigree. Having a stopper this good means the Grandmasters have practically bricked up their goal." Then the wall divides. And with good reason. "Flagrant Pongo Stinky Stinkman a.k.a. 'the Hermit' has got in between the defenders and is causing the visitors problems," shouts Bob excitedly.

"He hasn't had a wash in years - he's arguably the dirtiest player since Vinnie Jones played on a muddy pitch and the showers were broken," quips Ray. "And the Grandmaster players in the wall are shrinking away from his stink."

"And I can report all the flies in the stadium have just dropped dead," announces Bob.

"Think that's because of your aftershave, Bob," says Ray.

"The two German defenders Herr Kutt and Herr Dreyer are encroaching the ten metre line, Ray."

"That's right, Bob. But the ref's rightly having none of it. Not the first time the Germans have encroached into occupying somewhere they shouldn't be, right Bob?"

As Amadeo curves the ball in towards the goal, Mac the Keeper times his leap perfectly and jumps off the crossbar, landing on the back of the Grandmasters' keeper's neck.

Commentator Bob's voice rises a full octave in excitement: "Amadeo shoots. But a goalie this good, this superb, this reliable, should easily have it covered."

Only he does not seem to have it covered at all. Instead the Grandmaster stopper Saf Hans staggers about trying to get Mac off his neck, like someone desperately attempting to get rid of a bee inside their clothing. Consequently the keeper loses his balance, falls to the ground and the ball flies into the unguarded net.

"GOOOOOAAAAALLLLL!!!!" screams the crowd.

Lara and the foosballer players express their jubilation, yelling "Yesssssss!!!!!! GOOOOAAAAALLLLL!!!"

Mac jumps from the goalkeeper's neck and runs around in the six-yard box with arms outstretched as if he's scored the goal, courting teammates' congratulations. Commentator Bob summarises the action his eyes have just seen, but his brain is having difficulty processing: "Incredible. Utterly incredible. The rag bag team of Village no-hopers - and that was the kindest pre-match description we could find - have just scored!"

Realising that Bob is frozen in startled shock, Ray takes over broadcasting duties: "The Village team have scored. An inexplicable mistake by the butter-fingered, Vaseline-gloved, air-flapping dodgy keeper Saf Hans - as Ray and myself had just been describing him."

"Yes," agrees Bob with returning powers of post-shock speech, "Ray and myself were right to warn about that dodgy keeper."

The entire Village Team converge to celebrate the goal - with the lone exception of the Hermit who is making use of his stinky space on the far wing.

Once over his incredulity, commentator Bob is speaking rapidly into the microphone. "Who would have thought it? The Village are back in this. It's now Grandmasters 2 Village Team 1."

Ray concurs. "That's right, Bob. The wall parted like a 1950s footballer's hair - quite terribly. And the match is suddenly transformed. We were right to warn about that dodgy keeper though. How prophetic are we, Bob?"

Meanwhile Beville Beville helps Mac, who has slid out of the Grandmaster goalkeeper's shorts, and aids him off the pitch. "Are you all right, Mac?"

"It was horrible in there. I may need counselling."

Skip is inspiring his troops. "This game's far from over, boys. We need one more big effort."

Flash prepares to restart the game, insulting his teammates in the process. "Concentrate, you nobodies. Why must I do everything myself, just because I am the great anointed one who walks among you lowlife. Now concentrate, you overpaid, over-rated space-wasters."

Dark jerseyed Grandmaster Sacramerd exchanges a one-two with Flash and is about to find a teammate in a dangerous position, when the ball suddenly takes an unexpected bobble, leaving the Frenchman kicking fresh air and falling over on his derriere as a consequence. The invisible Loco has flicked the ball up, causing another bobble, and now places a measured side-foot pass to the Emo Kid. In turn, the Emo Kid finds the one Village teammate guaranteed to be in lots of space and completed unmarked. The Hermit in turn finds Moxey out on the wing. Known for his pacemaker rather than his pace, Moxey doesn't exactly fly down the wing. But every one of the three covering defenders bizarrely trips when attempting to close him down. The foosball players high-five each other in celebration.

Flash comes over and remonstrates bitterly with the fallen full-backs. "You'll never play for my team again, you imbeciles."

The Hermit lays off the ball to Spencer, who instantly loses it to an opponent. But the Village Team immediately regain possession, mainly because Skip, Gregor and two other foosball players pick up the ball and run off with it. Skip feeds the ball to the Emo Kid who distributes it brilliantly with the outside of his foot to Moxey.

"Marvellous skills from the bedroom boy there, Bob."

With the secret help of Rico, Loco and Beville, Moxey slips past one defender and eludes another. The first Grandmasters challenger misses the ball. Then a second would-be challenger is upended by an expert trip by Gregor – Gregor being the type of player hardly adverse to making a rash tackle whilst already on a yellow card.

"Unbelievable! And the second Grandmasters defender falls flat on his overpaid, over-exposed face!" summarises Bob. "He's gone down there like he's been hit by an anvil dropped from a crane," observes Ray.

Then it's back to the Hermit, who receives the ball in characteristic isolation and passes to Amadeo who is bearing down on goal. On the edge of the area Amadeo is brought down by a late clumsy challenge from defender Don Keyes.

Lying on the ground, Amadeo spots two tiny figures run past his field of vision right in front of his left eye. "Skip? Rico? What are you doing?"

"Oh, er, hi Amadeo," says Skip. "Me and the lads have been giving you a bit of help. I think we've turned it around. The Grandmasters have no idea what's going on."

Amadeo is firm and adamant in his response. "NO! No cheating in this game. We do it on our own. It doesn't matter if the opposition cheat or bribe - the game only means something if it's played honestly. And I intend to play honestly."

A disappointed Skip is surprised Amadeo is not more grateful for the foosball players' help. "What?! You lot don't stand a chance against these top pros. And Flash is cheating - that scything tackle he did earlier should have got him a season's ban at least - and probably named in an international arrest warrant!"

But Amadeo stands firm. "We'll do it our own way. On our own. Within the rules. Or it means nothing at all." He looks at the Village Team who are all standing around him, weary, out of breath but determined, Lara's rousing half time team-talk still buzzing in their ears. The Priest mops the sweat from his brow. The Emo Kid stares at his teammates with a look of icy determination. Gill Etre is advising the referee to book an optician's appointment at his earliest convenience. The Guv'nor is doing press-ups. Moxey has even put down his pipe to give the game his full concentration. The Hermit is breathing directly onto the Grandmasters' centre-half in an attempt to put him into an induced coma, while the Pickpocket remorsefully returns the referee's watch and notebook. Even Chester starts jumping around like a boxer. "Come on. It's glory time. Just coming up to Victory o'clock!" Chester picks up his cap and goes to put it on his head, but drops it. "Come on the Village, we can score. I know we can," he adds.

Skip looks at the motley group of Village footballers and realises Amadeo is right. Amadeo stands upright with a proud smile on his face. He winks appreciatively at Skip, a signal of gratitude to Skip and his boys. Skip puffs out his chest in pride, turns to face his men and Gregor's Clarets. "We've done our bit. Now it's time to hand over to the tall guys out there." The Stripes and the Clarets walk off the pitch, knowing they have won the battle, now it is up to the Village Team to win the war.

The match restarts. The Guv'nor thumps the free kick straight into the wall, which has the effect of flooring and knocking out cold one of the Grandmasters. The loose ball falls to Fast Fingers Flynn. Commentator Bob takes up the story: "the Pickpocket has been practically handcuffed to his marker all game. But he breaks free this time. He could yet steal this match for the village. He plays a quick one-two with the Policeman, then lobs a fine cross into the mixer."

As the ball comes back down, two defenders both go for it and get in each other's way. The mix-up in the defence between the two international German centre-backs allows the Emo Kid, now galvanised with determination, to reach the ball first. The Emo Kid launches himself into a header. He rises like a salmon with a jetpack. He heads home past the despairing dive of the Grandmasters' keeper. The crowd scream "GOOOAAALLLL!"

"It's two-all. Is it, Ray, is it really 2-2, Ray? IS IT 2-2??!!"

"Incredible scenes, Bob. I can confirm it is very much 2-2. Probably the first time ever the pasty Emo Kid has been on a football pitch - or even outside - and he's turned this game around."

"Where oh where were the Germans? And frankly, who cares?" asks commentator Bob.

"Er, that sounds familiar, Bob."

"Come on the Village... er, and the, er, Grandmasters too, but mainly the Village," says Bob, in a rare lapse from his neutral unbiased commentating self.

22

Lara can't believe it. Nor can many others in the stadium. The foosball players celebrate like they've won the League, FA Cup, World Cup and Conference North play-off semi-final with the same goal.

Commentator Ray analyses the goal that means it's now Village 2 Grandmasters 2. "The Pickpocket stole in there between them all, picked the full-back's pocket – in both senses of the phrase. Eventually leading to a really brave header by the Emo Kid - the pasty kid giving the favourites a pasting."

"That's right, Ray, and we should say as responsible broadcasters that if you have an Emo or Goth at home, then do bear in mind that if left inside parked cars in sunlight on hot days, Emos and Goths can die."

Even the TV director and technicians are celebrating. Only the Agent sits unmoved, seemingly lost in deep contemplation, his hands resting on his bulging stomach.

"The crowd has gone wild," reports commentator Bob. "It's an Emo-tional moment here. Real Emo-tion."

"Top punning punditry, Bob."

"As I'm sure you recall, Ray, Amadeo told us in a pre-match interview: 'There is no 'I' in 'team'.'"

"That's right. And I recall Flash replied: 'There's certainly an 'f' in 'freak' - I can see one right now'."

"I sure can, Bob."

Play resumes with the Village Team energized by their two goals. Newly invigorated with confidence, they press forward. A powerful punt from the Guv'nor breaks to Amadeo. The

Grandmaster keeper just manages to tip his first-time effort on goal round the post. "If the keeper had cut his nails last night, he wouldn't have reached it, Bob," jests Ray.

The action now switches to the other end. The Grandmasters are too fast for Spencer, Moxey and Gill Etre, and carve open the Village defence. Just as Amadeo braces himself to see the Village net bulge, Chester pounces and makes a brilliant save to his left.

"Fantastic save, Chester. Well played!" shouts Lara from the stand, lit up with pride for her brother.

Flash then blatantly elbows parish priest Father Dick Dawkins, yet the referee gives nothing. The crowd boo Flash.

The Pickpocket nicks possession again, picking up the ball and running with it before threading an inch-perfect pass through to the Emo Kid.

"There's not much time left on the clock for a winning goal, Ray."

The Emo Kid dribbles the ball past two opponents and skips past another with a skilful shimmy. "The gloomy teen is showing some deft touches out there on the park this afternoon," observes commentator Bob.

The whole of the Village Team are pushing forward. "The momentum is with the Village Team now. They're determined to win it. This is real David versus Goliath stuff," enthuses Bob.

"Yes, and we all know who won that day: Goliath undone by a shot from distance, Bob."

"Mesmeric, silky skills from the Emo Kid," observes Ray, as the pasty bedroom boy's hip-swivelling run sees him tearing into self-created space down the left flank. The Emo Kid puts his foot on the ball, deliberately draws in the tackle from the Grandmaster full-back, then skips past him with a tantalising burst of acceleration. Looking up, he places a pass of geometrical precision to the Guv'nor.

"That's a perfect pass by the Emo Kid - he's put that on a sixpence for the Guv'nor. The ball has got 'Tap-this-easily-into-the-net' written on it, Bob."

"Err… I think it actually says 'Mitre' on it, Ray."

Unfortunately the Guv'nor selects power over placement, and although his shot zooms towards the target faster than most heat-seeking missiles, accuracy is compromised by pace. It misses the goal frame by millimetres. "Ohhhhh… so close!" groan the foosballers under the bench, their tiny heads held in tiny hands.

Demonstrating a tireless, selfless work rate from the restart demanded by Lara's half time pep talk, the Pickpocket robs a hesitant Grandmaster. "That's probably the first time the Policeman has been pleased to discover him in possession," notes Ray. He finds the Policeman with a clever defence-splitting through ball. The stadium clock is now showing one minute to go. Amadeo gains possession from the Policeman's lay-off near the edge of the Grandmasters' penalty area. All of the foosball players are now furiously crossing themselves. Amadeo controls the ball and hits it on the volley. Surely his shot has the keeper beaten…

"It's going in. It must be. Yeeess…" implores Skip.

"He's hit the bar! How unlucky was that? Deserved to be the winner," says Bob.

"The woodwork is playing a blinder as the mainstay of the Grandmasters' defence, Bob."

Rebounding off the bar, the ball heads straight back to Amadeo who is unmarked in the penalty area. This is looking good for the Village Team, as Saf Hans, the Grandmasters' goalie, is still sprawled on the ground after diving fruitlessly to save the previous rasping shot. An open goal is winking at Amadeo. He is six metres out and surely cannot fail to tap the rebound into the gaping goal. The home fans stand up as one; this must be the winning goal. And how fitting that Amadeo will score it. And how deserved. The goal that will bring salvation to the village.

Calmly Amadeo remembers to keep his eye on the ball, leaning forward to keep it down - he doesn't want to appear on a

YouTube hit of "worst open goal misses ever". He steadies himself and is just about to stroke the ball into the open goal when…

"Arrrghhhh!!" Amadeo collapses with a loud, ground-shaking clatter like a felled redwood tree. His cry of pain is met by sinister laughing from Flash. Amadeo is clutching his leg, rolling on the ground in agony, because…

"Flash has blatantly kicked him on his standing leg just as he was about to despatch the ball goalwards for a simple tap-in!" commentates Bob.

"Unbelievable. Flash just kicked Amadeo in full view of everyone. It must be a penalty and a red card. But Bunga the referee waves play on. As does his assistant Flaggio 'The Bat' Pipistrello."

Skip yells from the bench: "A blindfolded dead bat who'd lost his glasses would have seen that from behind a fence ten miles away in the dark."

"Referee, *$*&!&^%$!!!" yells Loco, his calm Buddhist mantra suddenly deserting him.

"Oi, that's the most obvious penalty I've ever seen. Er… I mean Rico's ever seen… er… Rico means that Rico has ever seen." Such is his rage that Rico temporarily forgets to speak in the third person.

The Clarets and Stripes yell at the referee, loudly bemoaning the injustice everyone in the stadium has seen. Everyone, that is, with the crucial exception of Signor Bunga and his assistant Pipistrello.

"The officials are playing a blind-er," puns Ray.

The momentum of Skip's anger pushes him onto the pitch, and the other foosball players rush to restrain him. Also on the pitch the Village Team's players swarm around the referee to complain. Yet remarkably he continues to wave play on, refusing to discuss the incident. Remarkable because the materials that penalty was made from were cast iron and stone wall.

"The referee needs to read the following letters from an optician's chart: Y.O.U.B.L.I.N.D.G.I.T." advises Rico.

The priest Father Dawkins approaches Signor Bunga and suggests: "Referee, my blessed child, why don't you **** off you ****** ****? Peace be with you."

Gill Etre also expresses an unambiguous opinion: "Referee, I really must protest in the strongest possible terms as you really are an absolutely quite, quite, quite dreadful and beastly man," she states loudly and clearly in her best BBC Radio 4 continuity announcer's voice.

Then an even bigger injustice threatens to damage the Village side.

Delirious with rage, all the Village players are crowded around the referee appealing for justice. But as Amadeo lies prostrate on the turf, Flash runs at full pelt towards the Village's unguarded goal. The ball, it seems, has remained in play, despite the obvious foul and the protestations of the Village Team. Goalkeeper Chester is also absent, positioned in a goalkeeper's no man's land, pleading with the others for the most obvious penalty since the spot kick rule was introduced in 1891. The Village players, suddenly aware of Flash's attack on their unguarded net, scream for him to kick the ball out of play, allowing Amadeo to receive treatment. Any sporting footballer throughout the world would comply to this protocol - with the notable exception of Flash. He has no intention of selecting the sporting option.

Wearily Amadeo staggers to his feet, only to see Flash bearing down on goal. The crowd boo their disapproval. Flash, insensitive to such emotions, carries on towards the deserted goal. He holds his hands out as if waiting for applause. Amadeo picks himself up and at once realises that Flash has to be stopped. While his teammates continue to berate the match officials, he runs as fast as he can towards his own goal. Pounding the turf, he is driven in his single-minded determination to stop Flash stealing this game. This is no longer the Village Team versus Grandmasters. This has become Good versus Evil - the forces of hope, compassion, decency and justice… all the good qualities in the world bundled together and pitted against Flash - earth's representative for all things bad and unjust.

Flash slows down his charge towards the vacant goal - not because he has suddenly discovered moral decency and fair play, but in order to wave at the crowd, basking in what he misinterprets as their admiration. Meanwhile Amadeo is still to trying to stop him, running faster than he has ever run before.

Skip optimistically screams, "Offside! Surely, lino?!" at the referee's assistant Ricardo Yelocard. In a futile attempt to get the linesman's attention Skip repeatedly yells "Lino, lino, lino, lino, lino, lino!" like a man enthusiastically declaring his favourite type of floor covering.

But Flash is not offside. Moreover his route to goal is unblocked by any Village players. Consequently he slows down to a mere trot, and blows kisses to the crowd. Even by his standards of award-winning arrogance, this is damagingly show-off behaviour. Amadeo, meanwhile, is gaining ground. With every metre Flash advances towards goal, Amadeo is covering two. For the first time, the crowd sense a flicker of hope that Amadeo may get back in time. But it is only a brief flash of optimism dispelled by a Flash of despair. Amadeo gamely slides towards the ball, but fractionally too late as Flash deftly chips the ball over Amadeo's outstretched leg and it rolls slowly towards the net.

"But has Flash hit the ball hard enough? Will it have the legs to make it?" ponders commentator Bob. The ball rolls teasingly towards the goal-line then appears to stop.

"Remember all of the ball has to cross the line for a goal to be awarded."

"The ball appears to have stopped on the line. Flash has turned away to begin celebrating, But that's not a goal."

Like an approaching tube train, spectators initially register a slight breeze that suddenly turns into a strong gush of air. A gust of wind is suddenly felt approaching by the spectators.

Propelled by the cold blast, the ball causes the ball to make one last half-revolution.

The ball has crossed the goal line by two centimetres. A silence descends on the stadium. The scoreboard dutifully clicks to display: Village 2 Grandmasters 3. Elation has turned into despondency.

In the commentary box, a breathless Bob gasps: "Where's the defence? Where's the goalie? Where's the justice for the home side now? They're going to lose a game they should have won!"

A silence descends upon the stadium like a sudden chill. No-one is celebrating. Only the howl of the wind is audible in an area packed with thousands of spectators.

Then the silence is shattered by the referee blowing a shrill "Pheep-pheep-pheeeeeep!" on his whistle - the third and final "pheep" especially and horribly elongated.

"Think the ref may have trouble reaching the tunnel, Bob." "Presumably because of the controversy oh his last decision, Ray?" "No, because he's too blind to see the tunnel entrance."

Skip slumps down onto the bench, like an inflatable with a hissing leak. Several rows behind him, Lara mirrors his action.

Then Loco notices something. "Don't be deflated, dude. Skip, you just need to listen."

Skip is not happy. "This is no time to peddle your new-age claptrap slogans, Loco, it really isn't."

"No, Skip, I mean really listen. Just listen," implores Loco.

"To what? I can't hear anything," snaps Skip. "Exactly, Skip, exactly."

"Of course," says Skip, suddenly understanding what Loco is getting at. Lara has noticed this phenomenon too.

There are no cheers, no applause. The entire stadium is silent, empty of any celebratory noise.

Skip looks up in wonder. On the pitch, Amadeo looks distraught - felled by defeat. Flash is standing beside him, grotesquely arrogant, maniacal, jigging with delight, half-speaking, half-singing: "Ha ha ha. I won. Ha ha ha. I won. I won. Goal. GOAL! I did it. Ha ha ha. I did it. I am not a true great, I am THE true great. People will only call Messi and Ronaldo ordinary after they have seen me play."

And yet everyone seems to be ignoring Flash. Ever the determined narcissist, he cannot understand why. An unnatural fragile silence reigns in the stadium. Then, only faintly at first, voices are heard. The murmurs build; then quickly the stadium erupts into applause and celebratory singing. The crowd is chanting and applauding the defeated Village side's achievements, not the victors' hollow triumph. Lara runs down from her seat, leaps over the perimeter fence and approaches Amadeo. He is still crestfallen, lying prostrate in the centre-circle. "Let me through!" she shouts. "Amadeo! Amadeo!" She strokes his chin, but he remains disconsolate, crushed. "We lost, Lara. We lost. I'm so sorry."

"That doesn't matter, Amadeo. It really doesn't matter."

Amadeo continues to look heartbroken, on the verge of tears. "I've failed, Lara. We lost."

"You haven't failed, silly," says Lara. "Listen. Listen to the sound of the stadium! You've won the hearts of the crowd. And theirs aren't the only hearts you've won today." With that Lara wraps her arms around his neck and pulls him towards her. Their mouths meet in a long kiss.

Observing this embrace, the normally unemotional Skip comments: "Ahh, that brings a tear to the eye of an old cynic like me. And I don't even have a heart. Or tear glands."

But his attention is immediately moved from Amadeo and Lara by a grinning Gregor approaching him. "Hey, I've got an idea," proposes the burly Glaswegian defender, "I'd swap shirts with you but it's painted on." They both laugh. "Mind you, pink isn't my colour!" quips Beville Beville.

"Actually, guys, it's Claret - not Pink," declares Skip. "From now on, we should call them the Clarets." Gregor and Skip hug manfully.

The crowd is now demanding that the Village Team do a lap of honour, before exiting down the tunnel carrying Amadeo aloft. Rico follows them, blowing kisses to the crowd. "Rico's public adore him," he shouts to the others.

"Oh give it a rest, they can't see you. Which is just as well with that hairstyle," retorts Gregor.

Now there is a standing ovation throughout the stadium. The crowd are chanting for the Village, and for the Village alone. One of the Grandmasters comes over and asks to swap shirts with Amadeo. "Look, Bob. One of the Grandmasters wants to swap shirts with Amadeo."

"And now the other Grandmasters go up to the Village players to swap shirts as a token of appreciation of what they've achieved," broadcasts Bob.

"What lovely scenes... ahem... sorry, thought I was stronger... sniff," stammers Ray fragmentally between sobs.

"Even though they didn't win the match, the Villagers won the hearts of the crowd. For ninety minutes they made the impossible seem possible, Ray."

"Gallant display from the plucky part-timers. Caused the big boys more scares than a horror fest movie marathon weekend. That was some potential banana skin, and the trombonist was primed to blow the accompanying sound effects whenever they slipped," adds Ray.

"Er... yes, Ray. It certainly showed the capacity of the Beautiful Game to contain shocks."

"Responsible for more shocks than an unqualified electrician, Bob."

"Thanks, Ray," says Bob. And he privately concludes - in his thoughts not words broadcast on the airwaves - that his co-commentator Ray might consider some electro shocks himself. To the brain.

Ignoring this image, Bob continues: "The Village Team made the all-conquering Grandmasters look ordinary."

23

Bob and Ray continue to broadcast as they wait to go live for a promised pitch-side post-match interview with Flash that the Agent has earlier brokered. But there appears to be a delay in setting up the interview. Aspiring as usual to be the consummate broadcasters, Bob and Ray are filling in time.

"And I'm told that we'll be able to have an exclusive live chat with winning captain Flash any second now." "That's right, Ray. In the meantime a distinguished viewer Sir Lee Gitt has asked why sports commentators are always obsessed with statistics and often refer to baffling American sports."

"A bit harsh, Bob. That's only our 37th complaint in 212 games about stats overuse, which equates to only 17.45% and a 5.727 game/complaint ratio."

"So we've batted that accusation straight outta the ball park, Ray."

"We certainly have, Bob. And another viewer asks why do us pundits keep saying players need to dig deep to get themselves out of a hole?"

"Surely digging deeper would make it harder to get out of the hole?"

"Fair point, Ray. Apologies but I have to interrupt you there as I'm hearing we can now not hear from Flash… oh."

The Agent has cancelled Flash's TV appearance.

Uncharacteristically dejected, Flash stands alone in the middle of the pitch. He is unused to not being the centre of attraction, and he doesn't like it at all. Bizarrely he beckons to the crowd, placing his hands to his ears. "I can't hear your applause. Where's my applause then? Isn't anyone going to applaud me? It was me that won it. It was ME!!"

Applause for the Village team is by now with interspersed with jeers for Flash. "Boo... what a Flash git!" exclaims a spectator. The Agent shuffles slowly onto the pitch. His legs struggle to transport his generous frame, meaning that he moves precariously like a bear walking on its hind legs. He approaches Flash. "Sorry, Flash, the people don't want you anymore."

"What?! Then make them want me. That's what I pay you for, isn't it, numbskull?"

"Actually," begins the Agent, in a much calmer tone than Flash's, "you don't pay me anymore, Flash. Because I quit."

Flash is not a man familiar with being rejected.

The Agent speaks slowly, rather enjoying the taste of the words forming in his mouth. "Stars lose their brightness. Idols fall from favour. Agents are forever. You're yesterday's news. You're a Flash in the pan."

"What... wh... what... about...wh... wh..." Flash is forced into inarticulacy.

"Even the brightest stars one day collapse. You're a shooting star. Agents move on to the next star."

"What? Eh? No, I will not allow you to quit. I am Flash! Internationally known as 'A Soccer Superstar' People say it should be an acronym for me: 'ASS' - whatever that is... hey, come back here! You cannot quit, do you understand? I forbid it! It is so unfair. You must do as I say. Come back here!" Flash is sounding like a tantrum at nursery school.

But it is too late. Flash is unrepresented. His ex-Agent unrepentant. His public unresponsive. A man fallen from fashion and favour. And given the way he has treated people on the way up, the way down will almost certainly prove to be a very lonely and unfriendly place.

Then a beaming golden smile returns to the Agent's fat face. But it is definitely not directed at Flash. The Agent now has a different target for his sparkling smile: "Hey, Emo Kid, great silky skills out there today… how would you like to join one of the really big clubs and be a star? I can help you earn enough money to buy all the Black Veil Brides and My Chemical Romance CDs any Emo kid could possibly want."

A discarded banner blows across the stadium and lands on top of Flash, totally obscuring him.

24

Matty is tucked up in bed captivated by the story, radiant with intrigue.

"What happened next? Well? Go on, tell me," he demands. "What happened to Lara and Amadeo? Skip and Gregor. And what did Loco and Rico do? Dad, please tell me."

"It's ever so late, and your mother will be furious if she knows you're still awake."

"Please, dad," Matty implores.

"OK, then, I'll tell you. Everyone decided to build a brand new village rather than inhabit the architectural monstrosity that Flash had built. No one came to the Astro Dome Stadium and it became a white elephant. It was built on the cheap and soon started to crumble. The rusty gates have been padlocked for years as it isn't safe. Everyone made the most of an opportunity to make a new start in the rebuilt village. The Hermit now showers daily and is off the booze - but he's still a hermit who prefers to live miles and miles away from the club he supports – so that's why he can only be a Manchester United fan. He still plays for the Village side that was founded that fateful day. They have a good reputation in lower non-league football – no opposition relishes a visit to the Village's ground, Sewer Stink Lane with its famous slope. The Emo Kid has a successful career in top flight football as a natural goalscorer. He scored a famous hat-trick in a game that relegated the Grandmasters.

"And what happened to the Pickpocket Fast Fingers Flynn?"

"He went into politics."

"What about the other Village Team members? What happened to Spencer and Moxey?"

"They won the pools. They used their windfall to rebuild the café, insisting on every feature - even the football pennants on the walls - being recreated exactly to match the original. The Guv'nor still serves thirteen different types of chips."

"Wow. What happened to everyone else? Please tell me!" begs Matty. "I'll tidy my room tomorrow morning, I promise, if you tell me."

"Well, I'm not sure. It really is late. Maybe tomorrow?"

"Now, please. I'll take out the bins for a whole month."

"Hmm… that's definitely a deal we shouldn't decline," says his mother, appearing in the doorway and handing her husband another cup of tea. "I think now is the time to show him. School night or not, this is very important."

"Show me what? But what happened to Amadeo? Please tell me," insists Matty.

"Amadeo won Lara. That was the only result that mattered to him - turned out to be the only match he truly cared about. They married and had a son. A son who wasn't very good at going to sleep at bedtime," reveals his father.

"But a son who will be putting the bins out every day for the next month," says his mother.

"Week. I think I said a week," retorts Matty.

"Nice try, Matty, but a month it definitely is," says his mother firmly. "That is, of course, if you want to know what happened to the real Rico, Loco, Skip, Psy Kick, Gregor, Mac, Beville twins and the others AND meet them… otherwise, a week is fine."

"Yes, please! Yes, a month is OK, I suppose! How can I meet them?"

"Well," Matty's mother says to his father, "you realise we could have negotiated two months there!?"

"Yeah, sorry," Matty's dad replies.

"Your father can take you there now."

"Now? Brilliant! I'll get my coat," says Matty, sitting up flushed with excitement. Then he springs out of bed. "How far is it? Can I have sandwiches for the trip?"

"It's not far at all," says his mother, "so definitely no sandwiches."

"What? That close? Where are we going?"

"You'll see. Now follow me when you've got dressed," says his father.

25

Matty has never put on a dressing gown and laced up his shoes quicker. He bounces with enthusiasm across the back garden. "So you're finally getting to see inside the tiny room above the garage that I always keep locked," announces his father.

"You mean the room where you and mum go a lot when I'm watching television?" asks Matty.

"Er... yes, that one," says his mother, sounding uncharacteristically ruffled.

His father fumbles for a key, trying to decide which one fits in the inadequate light.

"I don't believe the story can be true, dad. Things like that can't possibly be true, can they? It's just a story, right?"

His father stoops so that his head is level with Matty's. "Whether you believe me or not, well that's entirely up to you."

This response surprises the boy. "Are you really saying that Skip, Loco, Rico - and Rico's hair - are all real?

"If you believe, then they are."

"Seeing is believing," adds his mother.

"That's right, Lara," says Amadeo, "seeing is believing."

"Lara? That's not your name, mum. You're Maria. Everyone calls you Maria."

"Before I left the village to go to art school I was known as Lara. It was a nickname that stuck - apparently I looked like action heroine Lara Croft. As nicknames go, I was flattered - so I encouraged people to use it. After all, some nicknames can be dreadfully cruel..."

"Oi, Candy Floss Head - that's what I'm going to be calling you from now on - stop preening and get on with the game." Gregor is berating Rico for not taking a throw-in quickly enough for his liking. "Amadeo, the Stripes are time-wasting again."

Amadeo makes a shrugging gesture to Gregor, "I'm supposed to be neutral, guys."

Matty is transfixed. "Wow, I can see them all. This is amazing. Rico's hair really is that awful."

"Hmmm... Rico is unsure whether he likes this new Mini-Me version of Amadeo."

"That's a foul!" shouts one of the Beville twins - no one's quite sure which one - at Gregor.

"What? I hardly touched him. You're a diver."

Skip notices that Amadeo has arrived. "Hey, Amadeo, book him for a foul." "Nonsense, Amadeo, book their diver for diving," insists Gregor.

"Behave Gregor, or I'll have to get my yellow and red cards out," says Amadeo sternly.

"Sorry, boss. But football's a wee contact sport, y'ken. I'm not the sort of player who, if I've knocked into someone, goes back to exchange insurance details - if you know what I mean, boss," says Gregor, but his attention is suddenly claimed by Skip picking up the ball.

"Hey, handball!"

Unsurprisingly Skip is having none of it. "You committed a foul. So it's a free kick to us."

"I did no such thing!" Gregor denies everything, folding his arms and looking away to the side with a look of coy innocence that he is incapable of pulling off convincingly.

Matty stands gazing at the tiny animated footballers. Battery operated floodlights bathe them in light, each player casting four shadows.

"To Rico. Pass it long to Rico. Because Rico is the one who scores all the goals."

"Nonsense, I'm this side's leading goalscorer," argues Skip.

Only Mac, the Stripes' goalkeeper, notices the father and son leave. He raises his hand in a goodbye gesture to Matty and Amadeo - and consequently nearly gets lobbed with a speculative long-range effort by the Clarets.

"Oi, keep your eye on the ball!" demands Skip. "Don't ever take your eye off the ball."

"We're a team, man," says Loco.

There are no stars without the Stripes.

About the Author

Richard O. Smith is the author of *The Man With His Head in the Clouds* (Signal Books, 2014) a historical biography of James Sadler, the first Englishman to fly, interwoven with a humorously candid autobiography ("Very, very funny" - Lucy Porter). His other books include: *Oxford Student Pranks* ("A jam-packed jamboree of jollity" – Dr. Lucy Worsley), *Britain's Most Eccentric Sports* ("Better than all 26 days of a cricket match" - Henning Wehn) and Amazon no. 1 bestseller in humour *As Thick as Thieves*, documenting true criminal ineptitude ("Made me think I should have considered a life of crime" - Hugh Dennis).

Richard is a Chortle comedy award winner, a former National Football Writer of the Year and regular columnist for the *Oxford Times*. He has written for *The Independent*, *When Saturday Comes*, BBC Radio 4's *The Now Show* and *The News Quiz*, BBC2's *Dara O'Briain's Science Club* and writes for several well-known stand-up comedians.